The Fluxus Movement

A Selective Annotated Bibliography of

Dissertations and Theses

Milo Avicenna

_____

Avicenna, Milo

The Fluxus Movement: A selective annotated bibliography of dissertations and theses/Milo Avicenna

p. cm.

1. Fluxus Movement- -- Criticism and Interpretation. I. Title.

N 6537 .F37

ISBN 1497425409

ISBN-13 978-1497425408

Table of Contents

1.) **Allan, K.**
Conceptual art magazine projects and their precedents.
Ph.D. dissertation, University of Toronto (Canada). 2004.

Conceptual art magazine projects (like their earlier twentieth-century predecessors and later related tendencies) are designed to function as art or art-like occurrences in printed magazines. Magazine projects are not reproductions of artworks that were constructed for other purposes but are, rather, artworks in reproduction. The projects that I deal with involve deliberate employment and/or disruptions of the conventions of magazine publications; they were designed to alter and reconfigure the readers' experience of the magazine as a form of communication as well as challenge their expectations of art and its possible manifestations. The publications studied include small-run, self-produced journals designed as complete clustered or interrelated artworks through to mass-market art magazines for which the artists were invited to contribute one or more pages, and where the pages were understood to function as either alternative exhibition spaces or as discussion forums for ideas about art. I examine the origins of magazine projects during the early years of the century in European Expressionist, Futurist, Dadaist, International Constructivist, and Surrealist periodicals of the teens to the late 1940s. I also discuss later precedents for Conceptual art in Fluxus and experimental writing of the 1960s. Subsequent chapters are studies of one of several distinguishable means that were employed for using the magazine format to produce and distribute artwork.

Examples of the use of each generalized approach are then analysed in detail to support this typology. To conclude the dissertation, I examine the relation between Conceptual art and aesthetics because it is frequently proposed that it somehow managed to avoid aesthetics altogether. I consider the aesthetic role of obstacles to sensibility in Conceptual art and the encounter with art being a kind of learning-like activity that expands both understanding and general awareness. With Conceptual art, the pre-given knowledge and circumstantial evidence surrounding an artwork become part of the work in extension. Context, history, and interpretation are externally embedded as fluctuating components of the work. I reach this conclusion by the theorizing of a lateral extension of artwork and artist functions. [Author Abstract]

2.) **Avant-Rossi, J.**
Michael Nyman: "The Man Who Mistook His Wife for a Hat".
M.A. thesis, University of North Texas. 2008.

Composer Michael Nyman wrote the one-act, minimalist opera The Man Who Mistook His Wife for a Hat, based off the neurological case study written by Oliver Sacks under the same title. The opera is about a professional singer and professor whom suffers from visual agnosia. In chapter 1, the plot and history of the opera are discussed. Chapter 2 places The Man Who Mistook His Wife for a Hat alongside a selection of minimalist operas from Philip Glass and John Adams. Chapter 3 contains a history of the Fluxus art movement and shows where Fluxus-like examples appear in the opera. Chapter 4 includes Nyman's usage of minimalism, vocal congruencies, and Robert Schumann as musical elements that convey the drama. [Author Abstract]

3.) **Bari, M. A.**
Mass media is the message: Yoko Ono and John Lennon's 1969 Year of Peace.
Ph.D. dissertation, University of Maryland, College Park. 2007.

In 1969, against the backdrop of the Vietnam War, multimedia artist Yoko Ono and rock star John Lennon instigated a series of idiosyncratic artistic events designed to spread a universal message of peace. What all these events had in common was the couple's keen desire to act as catalysts for change and their willingness to exploit their own celebrity to do so. They had just survived a scandalous year in London in a fishbowl of publicity where the popular press savaged Ono and Lennon's love affair and resulting separate divorces. Dealing with the insatiable media had become part of their everyday lives. Why not use this pervasive attention to publicize their own cause and carry their message of peace throughout the world? This simple premise launched a private peace campaign whose artistic message has achieved cult status in our popular culture. This dissertation examines how Yoko Ono and John Lennon's 1969 Year of Peace unfolded, how the media covered it at the time, and how people remember it today. By considering the couple's art events within the context of the 1960s and then following the path of certain images as they wend their way to the present, Ono and Lennon's art acts as a core sample of sixties culture and its legacy. My study situates this artwork against the backdrop of Lennon's megawatt rock star celebrity, within the spirit of Fluxus (of which Ono was a founding member), and in the context of the anti-war movement of the time. In a larger cultural sense, I use Ono and Lennon's art as a touchstone to explore ideas about gender and ethnicity, the sixties counterculture, the language of everyday life, the nature of celebrity, the psychology of marketing, the role of mass media in society, and the control and manipulation of imagery. [Author Abstract]

4.) **Bowen, D.**
Danger box: Fluxphotography and Martin Heidegger's phenomenology.
Ph.D. dissertation, The University of Rochester. 2004.

This project concerns artists who, working under the banner of Fluxus in the 1960s and 1970s, generated a performative and interdisciplinary approach to photography--what I call "fluxphotography." Fluxphotography discloses the material, perceptual, and durational aspects of photography while suggesting a query which this project takes up: can artists alter photography, as well as the subject produced by and for the camera, by changing the way viewers and makers engage with it? While Fluxus refigured photography by conceiving of it as an event rather than an object, I find the medium to be historically determinate; it carries its history with it, authorizing what can be imaged, as well as the very experience the image elicits in its viewer. My project examines the ways in which Fluxus struggled with this contradiction and, in doing so, produced a body of work that aids in the theorization of photography. This dissertation's ambition is two-fold. First, it seeks to fashion a rich genealogy for contemporary artists who engage with the technologically produced image as a perceptual and experiential activity. A second and related goal is to deflate the predominant understanding of technology as an "engine" that determines the socius. Instead, I argue that technology is a social activity. I find that Fluxus offers a means to engage with photography in a manner that reveals this, often at the cost of the photograph's beauty and permanence. Methodologically, I utilize Martin

Heidegger's thought in order to explore the implications of the work discussed. In his 1927 opus, Being and Time , Heidegger describes an inter-dependant relationship between human beings and equipmental objects. Yet, in his later essays, Heidegger conceives of technology as a dangerously limited form of revealing that holds sway, enfolding human beings within its logic. Ultimately, I argue that Heidegger's early articulation of equipmentality challenges his more global theory of technology and, by extension, certain overarching notions of visual technology that prevail today. At the same time, I find that Heidegger's seemingly oppositional theories, when thought jointly, act as a heuristic device for delineating the theoretical boundaries of fluxphotography without evacuating its subtlety. Throughout this dissertation, Heideggerian thought is placed in dialogue with fluxphotography such that each responds to and helps to define the other. [Author Abstract]

5.) **Brandon, K. E.**
A writerly reading of art: theories of authorship and artists' books, 1960-1980.
Ph.D. dissertation, The University of Manchester (United Kingdom). 2009.

This study examines the field of artist, books from Europe and the US in the 1960s and 1970s in conjunction with concurrent theories of authorship, arguing that the artists' book can be seen as an instance of the polysemic, intertextual and writerly text described in such theories. Beginning with the 1967 publication of Roland Barthes's essay "The Death of the Author" in the American "journal-in-a-box" Aspen, I trace the writerly through artists' books produced by conceptual, Fluxus and feminist artists in this period. Aspen provides a rich starting point for my study as it traces a network of connections between figures such as St. Phane Mallarm and Marcel Duchamp, whose work has often been cited as prefiguring the artists' book, artists who worked with the book or the printed page, such as Sol LeWitt, Mel Bochner, and Dan Graham, and the theories of Barthes. I demonstrate how other connections can be drawn between contemporaneous theories of authorship and artists' books. Of particular note is the emphasis that artists'; books place on the reader/viewer in completing the book, creating an environment where the distance between artist and audience is broken down. Via an examination of the work of artists such as Marcel Broodthaers, Lawrence Weiner, Dick Higgins, George Brecht, Carolee Schneemann, Suzanne Lacy, and others, chapters address: the reasons for the privileging of the work of Mallarm in both writing on artists' books and poststructuralist theory; the move towards the artist-intellectual in this period and the possible connections this has with the emergence of the artists' book; the viability of the artists' book as "democratic" art form; the importance of the field for women artists who used the space of the page to disseminate a feminist message to a wider and more diverse audience than the traditional gallery-going public. [Author Abstract]

6.) **Bright, B. T.**
No longer innocent: The book arts in America, 1960 to 1980.
Ph.D. dissertation, University of Minnesota. 2000.

"No Longer Innocent: The Book Arts in America, 1960 to 1980" traces the emergence of the artist's book in America during the sixties and seventies in its three manifestations: the fine press book, the deluxe book, and the bookwork. The discussion considers the characteristics of the artist's book and the issues it raises that stem from its dual nature, that is its identity as both book and art. Those issues include the art world's historical bias against craft, questions of rarity and value arising from works made in multiple copies, and the challenge posed to traditional artistic media by the artistic use of commercial printing technologies. In fact, this history broadens the portrayal of the artists of the period to encompass the role of an independent publisher, or even of an artist standing at a copier or offset press. Together with the discussions of specific books and artists, this history also considers the book arts' own institutional development, along with the related worlds of typography, trade book publishing and independent publishing. The discussion begins with two chapters that concern European and American precursors from the late nineteenth century up to 1960, followed by two chapters that focus on the U.S. artist's book in the sixties and seventies. This study investigates how the book affected art movements sympathetic to its properties and potential, as a site and source of art-making, and in particular it considers key artists' books that responded to a specific art movement, like

Pop, Fluxus or Conceptualism. In addition, this dissertation traces an identifiable trend from the mid-fifties that consists of artists who have chosen to work with books, simply from a recognition that the book is an artifact that can inhabit both private and public realms, a performative object that can enact an artist's ideal of directly addressing an audience one-on-one. [Author Abstract]

7.) **Concannon, K. C.**
Unfinished works and aural histories: Yoko Ono's conceptual art.
Ph.D. dissertation, Virginia Commonwealth University. 2000.

Through representative examples of her instruction paintings, music, advertising art, and performance this study looks very specifically at Yoko Ono's Conceptual art, its development between the years 1961 and 1968, and the question of its place in the history of art. Building upon previously published research by Alexandra Munroe and Reiko Tomii, and bringing new research on Ono's works for advertising media to the argument, this study shows her work to be among the earliest examples of what would later become known as Conceptual art. Ono's focused and consistently conceptual orientation places her at the vanguard of a movement that would only be defined as such in 1967, by which time Ono had been working conceptually for six years. Ono's work is examined within the context of a Conceptualism that emerges from Fluxus and Minimalism, from the circle of John Cage, and from Ono's own background in Eastern philosophy. The dissertation also includes a substantial bibliography, incorporating citations for newspaper reports of Ono's activities from all periods of her career. [Author Abstract]

8.) **Conn, R. E.**
Device: An exploration of interior and exterior space as an aspect of interactive sculpture.
M.F.A. thesis, Western Carolina University. 2010.

This thesis and accompanying exhibition is an investigation of the nature of observation and the importance of audience interaction and response when presented with a challenging art object. The objects or "devices" in this exhibit form a dichotomy of attraction and repulsion through the evocation of fear and curiosity. As aspects of this exploration the exhibit addresses the significance of the display space and how our awareness of interior and exterior defines viewer response and the observation processes. Through an examination of the protocol established by gallery convention I determine how to recontextualize the space to stimulate interaction with my work. This work also addresses the passive- active observation process and the relationship it has to both audience perception and the definition of a contained space. With references to the Fluxus movement and the work of artists Allan Kaprow, and Robert Morris, this thesis addresses art that requires active investigation and participation by the viewer in order for the work to be complete. Devices created for the exhibition challenge interaction and manipulate the observation process of the audience. These devices function as private interactive spaces dividing the gallery into interior and exterior spaces. Integrated into each device is a canvas enclosure that allows for only one participant at a time to experience the interaction. Within these cells or personal refuges the viewer is challenged by the nature of this restrictive/contemplative space and his or her relationship to it. My work relates to that of Gregor Schneider in his manipulation of the domestic space with the inclusion of the human form. I also find connections to my work in the works of Bruce Nauman and Arthur Ganson. The gallery space in conjunction with the devices divides active from passive viewers. Active viewers or participants access the interior of the devices and interact with the mechanisms that are hidden beneath the canvas enclosure. This same enclosure forms the interior space and creates the divide from the common space of the gallery. The active participant is also limited to observation of the interior of the space and to the events created by the mechanism, which he or she may operate. This mechanism is only visible to them. The exterior of the device and the explicit effect of its operation are visible only to the passive viewers. From the exterior, the passive viewer receives only information that passes through the shroud via sound, movement against the fabric or those elements that penetrate the fabric all together. The same shroud that masks the mechanism and creates the private display space hides the head of the active participant. As a result of this integration of participant and sculpture the active participant will appear as an inextricable part of the device to those viewing from outside. It is my intention that the viewer become aware of the container or space into which each event is occurring, the private space of each device and the container of the gallery space as a whole. Ultimately these devices become proxies for me. As a result they become representative of the vulnerable nature of my art making process. The fear and curiosity response by the viewer is reflected back by the object and is emblematic voyeuristic relationship between artist and viewer. [Author Abstract]

9.) **Conway, M. T.**
Disorientations: Recovering the aesthetic in Queer Studies.
Ph.D. dissertation, Temple University. 2001.

A dual impulse underwrites much of Queer Studies. On the one hand, critics detail the derogatory treatment by which sexual minorities are subject to inequality. On the other hand, critics celebrate that which makes homosexuals unequal--their queerness--and argue that the difference marks a superior, not equal, subject-position. These protests against oppression and celebrations of a superior deviance are the orienting conceptual pair of Queer Studies. Unlike Gay and Lesbian Studies, Queer Studies is not exclusively concerned with homosexuality, but is instead interested in divergent thought and aesthetic practices considered more generally. While Queer Studies' celebratory and derogatory impulses dovetail with civil rights struggles, an exclusive focus on policy petrifies inquiry and aesthetic practices. This dissertation asks what would happen to these orientations if they were unhinged from political aims? Indeed, could Queer Studies imagine not strategizing, as a strategy? This dissertation aims to recover queer artifacts lost to the political imperatives of Queer studies, and to demonstrate the futility of relying squarely on political/juridical discourse to articulate what is ecstatic and what is tragic about queer artifacts and experiences. The aesthetic can be a resource for understanding those conflicts which can't be understood in the political realm, and for not reconciling those conflicts. This dissertation is interdisciplinary in methodology and in the selection of texts. The chapters investigate the dual impulse in a travel narrative centered on a homophobic homicide; two lesbian produced porn videos; and a Fluxus wedding performance. Each chapter is a case study of how the celebratory or derogatory impulse drives (or rarely, does not drive) the results of inquiry or aesthetic practice and what gets lost with those orientations. [Author Abstract]

10.) **Drukman, S. C.**
Junk theatre: Tracing the found object on stage.
Ph.D. dissertation, New York University. 2000.

This dissertation names and claims a genre called "junk theatre," a form of avant-garde performance that began with Marcel Duchamp and the Dada and Futurist movements and continues in American contemporary drama and performance art. By tying aesthetic and philosophical strands between artists who are not always grouped together, this study extracts new meanings from these artists' works. By drawing upon recent historical accounts of the avant-garde, this dissertation also offers a new way of understanding reiterated and recuperated styles throughout this century. This study owes much to Hal Foster's recent book The Return of the Real . His chronological re-marking of (roughly speaking) the 30s, 60s and 90s as three discrete but imbricated strands of avant-garde art is most persuasive. This chronology not only allows for finding historical markers, it argues that particular aesthetic and philosophical goals are both predicted and invoked retroactively by avant-garde artists. It refutes certain postmodern pessimists who maintain that recent transgressive art is only a pastiche or stylistic mimicry of past movements. Using this historical and theoretical framework helps establish junk theatre as a bona fide American avant-garde genre. After locating the origins of the "Junk aesthetic" in the ready-mades of Marcel Duchamp, this study draws connections between the Happenings and Fluxus artists like Joseph Beuys, between Paul Zaloom and Blue Man Group and between the work of Jack Smith and Richard Foreman. In fact, where Foreman is concerned (when so many theories have been used to cut into his enigmatic, layered theatre work), the lens of junk theatre provides a formalistic approach rarely used, and one that has the explicit support of Foreman himself. The oeuvre of Richard Foreman provides both a chronological and theoretical "bridge" between the 60's junk theatre (the neo-avant-garde) and the 90's junk theatre (the postmodern). In this last period, the plays of Mac Wellman and W. David Hancock are given close readings. [Author Abstract]

11.) **Dumett, A.**

Corporate imaginations: The Fluxus collective in the age of multinational capitalism.
Ph.D. dissertation, Boston University. 2009.

This dissertation examines the artists' collective known as Fluxus as it emerged within postwar multinational capitalism on three continents from 1962 to 1978. Fluxus's founder was the Lithuanian-born artist George Maciunas, who made organizational claims for the group--what I call his "corporate imaginations." I argue that for all its criticality, Fluxus also ambivalently shared aspects of the rising corporate culture of the day. My project focuses on the "business" of Fluxus, but more than that it concerns the larger discursive issues of organization, systematization, communication, and control that Fluxus both manipulated and set in relief. A cluster study of three crucial Fluxus artists--Maciunas, Korean-born Nam June Paik, and American-born Alison Knowles--reveals that through their performances and objects each developed historically specific strategies, appropriating tools and operations of the corporate system itself, as the system was understood at the time: an integrated set of economic, production, and personnel protocols. In chapter one, I describe the Fluxus strategy as "performing the system." Chapter two examines how Maciunas took up organization as a means to mimic the system's flows of production, distribution, and consumption in order to "flux" (purge) the system at every point. Chapter three looks at the various ways Paik attempted to "shock the system"--from his early performances in which he staged himself as the "yellow peril" to his more understated electronic works that took over dominant channels of communication for his disruptive feedback. Chapter four discusses how Knowles adopted systematic routines, ritualizing the mundane and monotonous to reveal not only the aesthetic structure of daily life but also the gendered terms of labor within an increasingly service- and leisure-based economy. Ultimately, these were strategies for becoming conscious critical subjects of multinational capitalism: via aesthetics of organization (Maciunas), communication (Paik), or routinization (Knowles). From the artists we learn that these strategies require a continuous, ongoing process of negotiating new relations of power and control within the totalizing, if flexible, nature of postwar capitalism. [Author Abstract]

12.) **Eisenstadt, E. J.**
The making of a "Livre de Lux" and artists' books in America, 1960 to 1982.
Educat.D. dissertation, Columbia University Teachers College. 1984.

This project consists of two separate sections, both relating to artists' books. This first section is an essay discussing various types of artists' books from 1960-1982. European antecendents are looked at and the role printed matter played in the Dadist, Futurist, and Russian Constructivist movements. The Fluxus movement, which was global, increased interest in the artists' book in America. Both literary and visual artists are involved in making artists' books. Several definitions of the artists' book are examined. Various methods of printing artists' books are discussed and the aesthetic criteria used by artists in choosing their technique. These include inexpensively reproduced works made on copy machines to the expensive hand-crafted livre de lux. General categories of artists' books are established and detailed examples given. Some of the categories viewed are manifestos, documentation of performance art, book as unique art object, and artists' notebooks. Aesthetic concerns in dealing with the artists' book such as linear time, sequential pages, repetitive image, and multiple copies are discussed. Descriptions of various presses are given and sources of artists' books are listed. The second section is an artists' book which I constructed and designed, which falls into the category of a livre de lux. The story selected was Jorge Luis Borges The Circular Ruins. It was chosen for its personal significance to me and because the images his words conjured up related to my painting. The book is a seven inch square with all images and text fitting into a five inch square. The text is hand-printed on a letterpress and the type is Century Schoolbook. There are eight colored etchings in each book which is hand bound in Italian silk and linen. There is an edition of fifteen. I was concerned with the visual and tactile aesthetics in creating a fine crafted work. I wished to devise my own illusion of Borges' vision. [Author Abstract]

13.)   **Fredrickson, L. J.**
Kate Millett and Jean-Jacques Lebel: Sexual outlaws in the intermedia borderlands of art and politics.
Ph.D. dissertation, Duke University. 2007.

This dissertation argues for the historical importance of two understudied artists of the 1960s, and beyond: Kate Millett, an American radical feminist, and Jean-Jacques Lebel, a French anti-Algerian War activist who went on to lead in the student/worker movement of Paris 1968. Both are artists, writers, and theorists who critiqued prevailing morés and celebrated a morality of libertine sexuality. This study explores their multiple activities and the ways in which each linked cultural and political avant-gardes. In doing so it sheds light on the contributions of experimental artists and their international and interdisciplinary circles to broader social developments. This dissertation has a tripartite structure. Firstly, it is grounded on close examination of the art and writings of Millett and Lebel. Secondly, it presents a theoretical argument for the convergence of three tendencies that shaped politicized art in the 1960s: an insubordination inspired by Dada, an ethics of committed action reflecting philosophical Existentialism, and a utopic belief in the revolutionary potential of liberated sexuality. Thirdly, it gives a historical reading of the transnational cultural circles in which Lebel and Millett worked in order to consider the evolution of avant-garde intermedia, art that operates between traditional media. This dissertation concludes that, despite differences in perspective regarding gender, sexuality, and the means that these artists use to radicalize their audiences, Millett and Lebel had certain critical similarities that made them icons of the 1960s: artistic backgrounds, shared morality of dissent, and individual lives of committed acts. This theoretical and historical work contributes to the history of experimental art, especially of Fluxus and happenings, and enriches understanding of the foundational practices of much contemporary art as well as scholarship on the interrelationship of culture and politics. [Author Abstract]

14.) **Goldberg, M. L.**
Reconstructing Trisha Brown: Dances and performance pieces, 1960-1975.
Ph.D. dissertation, New York University. 1990.

This dissertation is a description and analysis of works made New York City choreographer Trisha Brown during the early years of her career. Chapter one begins with Brown's childhood exposure to dance and athletics and continues with her West Coast studies at Mills College and Ann Halprin's studio. Chapter two and three focus on Brown's work in improvisation with the Fluxus and Judson Dance Theater groups in Greenwich Village in the sixties, highlighting the influence of composer John Cage and choreographer Merce Cunningham. Chapter four concerns Brown's critique of gender roles in autobiographical performance art works, often presented in museums. Brown utilized film, objects, and constructed costumes to present memories from adolescence or images from her life as a mother. Chapter five covers Brown's "equipment dance" series and the special floors and walls she engineered to dance in unusual relationship to gravity, emphasizing the interdependence of dancer and surround. Chapter six describes Brown's minimalist investigations into mathematical structure and her innovations in movement release techniques in the "accumulations." In these dances she superimposed externalized, machine-inspired choreographic "scores" and the sensual, unrestricted body. Goldberg intersperses dance description with insights from philosophy, literary and film theory, ecological psychology, and the visual arts. Inspired by the new ethnography, the manuscript is experimental in its spatial design: it is divided into various "textual voices" which, in their layout on the page, bring into contiguity documentary materials, theoretical contemplation, quotations from Brown and other artists, and personal reflections of the author about the process of creating a biography out of the artifacts of Brown's life. Goldberg writes as a younger choreographer who analyzes the work of her artistic predecessor. She grapples with issues of memory and history, and with the impact of the electronic machine--the computer or the video recorder--on the transmission of information. The resultant text features extensive live interview sources along with documentary materials and choreographic analysis, juxtaposed so that the sensual and the theoretical come into closer relation than is usual in dance scholarship. [Author Abstract]

15.) **Gonzalez, J. C.**
The paradox of John Cage.
M.A. thesis, Florida Atlantic University. 1992.

It has been said that John Cage has had a greater impact on world music than any other American composer in the 20th Century. His work spans the media of visual art, dance, literature, and most relevant to this study, theater. What seemed to be a troubled personal state in his life led him to Eastern philosophies. The Zen philosophy of non-intention led to the creation of music that expressed no emotion and allowed the audience to do its own listening. Moreover, this indeterminacy allowed music to be action. This theatrical approach influenced a generation of artists that became the heart of the anti-art movement. This movement included happenings, multi-media works, and Fluxus. Many of these events were not only a revolt against conventional art, but also the state of political and social thought. In attempting to say nothing in his works, Cage communicated his manifesto quite well. [Author Abstract]

16.) **Harren, N. O.**
Objects Without Object: The Artwork in Flux, 1958-1969.
Ph.D. dissertation, University of California, Los Angeles. 2013.

This dissertation examines the late-20th-century transformation of the art object through the practice of Fluxus, an international, neo-avant-garde artist collective founded in 1962 and centered in New York. Focus is given to three key figures: George Maciunas (Lithuanian-American, 1931-1978), George Brecht (American, 1926-2008), and Robert Filliou (French, 1926-1987). It traces chronologically these artists' development of three central Fluxus formats--the event score, Fluxbox multiple and Fluxshop--as they confronted established object categories pertaining to the mediums of music, painting, and sculpture; the emergent category of the multiple; and prevailing economic models of the commodity and the store/gallery. Fluxus was informed by the aesthetics of music, in particular the work and teaching of experimental composer John Cage. Chapter 1 thus provides an historical analysis of graphic notation in the 1950s in order to fully articulate the implications of the score model taken up by Fluxus artists in 1958--here seen as the foundational "diagram" for the Fluxus object. Chapter 2, focused on Brecht, examines the interrelation between the artist's event scores and object practice centered on readymade objects, here newly defined as "notational objects." Chapter 3 turns to Maciunas's production of Fluxbox multiples and that format's relationship to the medium of sculpture, the emergent market for artist multiples, and 1960s commodity culture, elaborating a theory of the

Fluxbox as "transitional commodity." Finally, Chapter 4 considers the aesthetic and political potential of Fluxus's "unworking" by the late 1960s through experimental forms of distribution and community-building modeled in the under-recognized work of Filliou. The project thus moves from an articulation of the origins of Fluxus's unique object model to a theorization of how the group's "objects without object" (to borrow the title of a work by Filliou) amounted to a radical statement about postmodern subjectivity and community formation. It provides a new account of Fluxus and of a crucial moment within the paradigm shift in postwar artistic practice toward the conceptual, ephemeral, and performative art forms that have come to define the post-medium condition of postmodern and contemporary art. [Author Abstract]

17.) **Hart, J. E.**
The will to theatre.
Ph.D. dissertation, State University of New York at Buffalo. 2000.

The Will to Theatre is an analysis of the genre of conceptual performance art in its relationship to and difference from the history and mimetic practice of drama and experimental theatre. The method of analysis focuses on the interdisciplinary relationship between the semiotics of Charles Sanders Peirce, psychoanalytic theory, Mikhail Bachtin's concept of the dialogic, experimental theatre and theatre history, art history, music and dance history, literary analysis and critical theory as they are applied to examples of Dada-based conceptual performance. Specifically, The Will to Theatre uses concepts of the indexical sign and the subjunctive mode to explore the dynamic of absence/presence operating in a total of 15 post-Dada performance pieces and two experimental plays. These concepts are initially developed in Part I, based in an examination of the 1970's performance work of Chris Burden, the 1960's Fluxus work of Ben Vautier, and the important and groundbreaking work by Dada master Hugo Ball at the Cabaret Voltaire in 1916. Part II focuses on two experimental theatre pieces, Breath by Samuel Beckett and a piece from Augusto Boal's Invisible Theatre series. These are followed by an analysis of individual pieces by artists: John Cage ("4'3 3"); Faith Wilding ("Waiting"); Vito Acconci ("Seed Bed"); Elizabeth Streb (reenactment of Yves Klein's "Leap into the Void"); James Luna ("Artifact Piece"); Karen Finley (two pieces from "The Constant State of Desire" series);

Diane Spodarek ("Codpiece"); and Adrian Piper ("Calling Card). Interspersed in the analysis of these pieces is commentary on and by artists Tristan Tzara, Bertold Brecht, Antonin Artaud, Alan Kaprow, Jackie Apple, Dick Higgins. Robert Morse, Yvonne Rainer, Carolee Schneemann, Cindy Sherman, Yoko Ono, and Joe Gould. <u>The Will to Theatre</u> attempts to construct a model for the consideration of an art form in which artists do not make art but become art through modes of contingency and direct address. This model argues, first, that post-Dada performance, based on the index, is functionally separate from the codes of theatre based on the icon of mimesis. The function of the index in performance signifies an existential and causal relationship between the sign and its referent; while the icon of theatre functions in an imitative relationship. Theatre mirrors events in the off-stage world; while conceptual performance, through the mixing of art and life, is an event. Secondly, while theatre and performance share aspects of the subjunctive mode - the presentation of the conditional *a s-if* - theatre concentrates on the *a s-if* of character while conceptual performance presents the *a s-if* of self. Simply, according to Stanislavski, Theatre presents a whole character created by an actor that uses his whole self as its basis. Theatre generally performs a knowing self-presence, one in which the actor produces the character out of him/herself. Performance presents the subject -as-process, never whole or totally present to him/herself; a subjunctive presence that finds itself part of an already ongoing reality, the stager of contingent processes, absence and doubt. Theatre separates performance from praxis, art from life; performance attempts to in-mix them. Examples. Chris Burden "disappeared" one weekend in 1971. He does not inform anyone that he is going or that he has returned. He announces his disappearance, a few days after he has returned, but without saying that his weekend had any special or artistic content. In his piece, he went about his usual weekend routine. The artist subjunctively creates everyday life in Southern California. The audience for Burden's disappearance does not know it is an audience. In contrast the audience for John Cage's musical composition "4'33"" knows very well that it is an audience. What they don't initially understand is that their incidental noise, as they sit in the auditorium waiting for the pianist to stop raising and lowering the piano cover, is the music as conceived by the composer. The audience is the music. Cage is responsible for introducing a whole generation of young artists in the 1950's and 60's to the neglected history of Dada performance first presented nightly in Zurich at the Cabaret Voltaire. The impresario for those first Dada evenings was Hugo Ball, who gathered around him several fellow exiles to create events that, I argue, have to be considered the first real performance art. Ball's "sound poems," influenced by Kandinski and German expressionist theatre, set the tone of early Dada. With his "sound poems" Ball attempted to transcend all sign systems, including language itself, as a way of attempting to escape from the dread brought about by the World War. I argue that his failure at transcendence, and his in-process discovery of contingency, doubt and absence significantly contributes to the beginnings of conceptual performance. One lesson from Ball, one that made him very unhappy, emphasizes that humans are elements (signs) that are part of semiotic systems that cannot be transcended. It was Ball's audience that apparently forced him to acknowledge this condition. Audiences are crucial for performance, for it is the agency of audience that complete and concretizes the work that the artist puts into play. The dialogical relationship with the audience is what literally makes the presence of the artist viable in the process of the performance, makes the subjunctive and the conditional presence of the event have significance. Performance is for the other. In the history of post-Dada theatre the lesson from both Brecht and Artaud is that it is the audience that makes meaning. In Diane Spodarek's "Codpiece" she dresses herself as a male homosexual and performs as such as a member of the nightly crowd in a gay leather bar. After three weeks, she ends the piece because her "audience" is not interested in becoming fellow performers. She does not get picked up. In this instance, her audience response in ignoring her reinforces the idea of the piece that gender itself is performed, and that maybe she was not performing her new role very well. Spodarek's piece is one of those, like Budren's or Ball's or Cage's that have acquired reputations based upon rumor and gossip. In some very important ways rumor and gossip are the primary means of documenting performance. Rumor and gossip extends the audience of the initial piece to include those not present at the initial event. The audience activity of hearsay re-performs the original, incorporating it in a process of extended discourse that itself becomes the piece. Here, art is no longer the sole origin and source, the cause leading to effects; in the extended discourse the original becomes an effect of the copy. The Will to Theatre explores this mode of documentation, comparing it to other forms of documentation, film, video and photography. Conceptual, post-Dada performance is based on absence, disappearance, a subjunctive presence that occurs in dialogical relationship with an audience. (In Ecrits Lacan says, "I identify myself in language but only by loosing myself in it like an object."(86)) But it is the history of drama and the activity of mimesis in theatrical performance that most shadows conceptual performance. Even though dada-based performance attempts to be deliberately non-mimetic, theatre and performance are part of a continuum. Every sign, according to Peirce, is tripartite: containing symbolic, iconic and indexical functions. Issues of theatre and theatricality can be, at least in contrast, a way of understanding performance. [Author Abstract]

18.)   **Higgins, H. B.**
Enversioning Fluxus: A venture into whose fluxus where and when.
Ph.D. dissertation, The University of Chicago. 1994.

This dissertation tells the story of Fluxus, the performance and object multiples group founded in 1962, using the critical, art historical, and mass cultural contexts since its inception. The fit or lack of fit between Fluxus and these contexts determines how it has been evaluated and represented through the present. I show how popular conceptions from the 1960s influence the present reception of Fluxus, and offer some explanation for why Fluxus has surfaced in the last few years in the journalistic and exhibiting mainstream. This explanation takes the form of a reception history of Fluxus, which is constructed from articles, exhibitions, and popular influences. Recent reception of Fluxus in the United States is based largely on a misreading of its past as uniformly leftist, formally revivalist and consensually organized, a problem sometimes exasperated by the artists themselves and indicative of the complex social organism of Fluxus. In contrast, following the initial identification of Fluxus as a resurgent Dada, much recent German reception has identified the group as politically and stylistically varied. The changing critical models of each location are explored in a comparative approach to differing definitions of Fluxus by site. Most theories of the avant garde postulate a slow absorbtion by the art establishment of avant-garde ideas, which are then in turn absorbed into the mainstream and transformed into kitsch or popular culture. Fluxus is interesting in this regard because, although Fluxus was not absorbed into the New York gallery world at its earliest moment, other conditions of mass culture were amenable to it. Examples include the political activities of John Lennon and his Fluxus artist wife, Yoko Ono, the video experiments of Korean artist Nam June Paik, which eventually lead to the development of technology used for MTV, and the Fluxhouse Cooperative development of Soho as an artist's neighborhood, which became the model for industrial loft conversions elsewhere. [Author Abstract]

19.)   **Kang, T.**
Nam June Paik: Early years (1958-1973).
Ph.D. dissertation, The Florida State University. 1988.

The achievement of Nam June Paik, commonly known as "the father of video art," has been recognized by several one-man exhibitions and accompanying exhibition catalogues in addition to numerous articles. But there is no systematic study of his development as an artist yet; Paik scholarship remains in a critical void. This is especially true for his early period when he was less publicized. The purpose of this dissertation is to portray him in the context of the artistic milieu from which he emerged as an established artist, and to relate his activities to broader art historical discourse. Paik was influenced by Kurt Schwitters, Marcel Duchamp, and especially by John Cage during his German period when he began his career as a performance artist associated with Fluxus artists. Cage's frontal attack on tradition and a negation of any value or taste in art were important lessons to Paik. Paik's "invention" of video art in the late sixties reflects the rise of dematerialized and process-oriented art at that time. The production of the Paik/Abe Video Synthesizer itself was an important contribution to video art history and it was aligned to his belief that video would replace painting. Influenced by McLuhan's global village idea, Paik focused on the information and communication side of video in the early seventies. The close formal and iconographical investigations of the three tapes The Selling of New York, The Global Groove, and A Tribute to John Cage reveal his aesthetics and working principles. The Global Groove established the norms of broadcast videotape and influenced many younger video artists. The characteristics of Paik's works such as an extensive use of kitsch, appropriation and recycling, a high degree of audience-consciousness, and rapid and discontinuous break in timing are all related to the features of Postmodernism. Paik is a quintessential Postmodern artist, and his future task is how to maintain the critical edge while fully embracing the popular culture. [Author Abstract]

20.)   **Kemp-Welch, K.**
Figures of reticence: action and event in east central European conceptualism, 1965-1989.
Ph.D. dissertation, University of London, University College London (United Kingdom). 2009.

The thesis offers a history of conceptual art as a vehicle for politicised action that goes beyond ideas of institutional critique and identity politics. It articulates a series of figures that relate to Vaclav Havel's essay 'An Anatomy of Reticence' through close readings of the practices of five artists, from Poland, Hungary, and former Czechoslovakia. Taking as its basis an expanded definition of conceptual art that incorporates action-based practice, the thesis compares disinterestedness, fidelity, ambivalence, doubt, and neutrality as critical positions adopted by artists in relating to late socialist realities. A pursuit of truth that shares a great deal with that outlined in the writings of Alain Badiou on the Event emerges as key to drawing out the traffic between these practices. Chapter one reads Tadeusz Kantor's Theatre of Events as a subversion of the Western trope of the Happening, with reference to Mikhail Bakhtin's definition of Carnival. Chapter two explores how Jerzy Bere's Manifestations can be read as a form of fidelity to the Event of Duchamp's readymade strategy. Chapter three analyses the collision of affirmation and negation in the ambivalent figure of irony, through the Joy and Zero actions of Endre Tót. Chapter four is concerned with doubt in the work of Július Koller, as against his paradoxical investment in the idea of the UFO. The final chapter considers in detail the

minimal actions of Jii Kovanda, and seeks to go beyond the conceptual binaries that emerged in the preceding chapters, by a discussion of Roland Barthes' definition of the Neutral. The conclusion proposes that the trope of Neutral was in many respects the paradigmatic 'figure of reticence' for the unofficial actions carried out in the time-frame of the thesis, which spans the period from 1965, when Happenings took over from Fluxus in the region, to 1989, when Communism in East-Central Europe, and the Cold War, ended.
[Author Abstract]

21.)   **La Bash, H.**
Yoko Ono: Transnational artist in a world of stickiness.
M.A. thesis, University of Kansas. 2008.

This thesis examines Yoko Ono and her work in relation to Fluxus from 1958 to 1964. Using theories of transnationalism, cosmopolitanism and performance to analyze discourse, I argue that Ono's hybrid Japanese and American identity as well as the Zen Buddhist elements of her work played into her acceptance in Fluxus and affected the reception of her work both by American and Japanese audiences. While Ono's membership reinforced American Fluxus members view of Fluxus as a transnational group, I argue that the group is better understood as cosmopolitan and operated in a geo-politically bound westernized, industrialized set of countries. Finally, I examine Ono and Fluxus in relation to the 1960's cold war environment, showing how some works were meant to create communitas, in response to that political climate. [Author Abstract]

22.) **Labelle, B.**
Background noise: sound art and the resonance of place.
Ph.D. dissertation, University of London, Birkbeck College (United Kingdom). 2005.

Since the early 1950s sound as an aesthetic category has gained prominence. Initially through the experimental music of John Cage and musique concrete, divisions between music and sound stimulated adventures in electronics, field recording, and the specialization of sonic presentation: musical composition was to take on a broader set of terms which often left behind traditional instrumentation and the control of the composer's hand. From this historical beginning, "Background Noise" follows the developments of sound as a specific artistic medium. Such chronology is informed by a thematic thread related to architecture, place and space: how does sound embed us within local environments? What consequence does sound-practice have on notions of spatially and architecture? Can we identify questions of identity and experience in relation to listening and the resonance of space? Chapter 1 explores the work of John Cage with the aim of identifying how sound was to become a distinct category. Oscillating between sound as worldly phenomena to music as cultural work, Cage sets the stage for a heightened consideration of listening and the "place" of sound. Specific works, such as 4'33" and Black Mountain Event, are investigated and compared to musique concrete and the Japanese performance group Ongaku, with the intention of underscoring their works as progenitors of sound-art. Chapter 2 sets out historically to follow Cage's influence in the works of Fluxus, Minimalist sculpture and music, and Conceptual art. The artistic developments of the 1960s introduce questions of phenomenology and presence alongside social and political concerns, demanding that art become indistinguishable from life. Robert Morris, La Monte Young, and Michael Asher use sound in diverse ways each of which points toward the potential of the medium to perform conceptually and phenomenally. Chapter 3 moves into Performance art of the early 1970s, addressing the works of Vito Acconci and Alvin Lucier, along with the contemporary work of Christof Migone, with the intention of hearing how the voice is used to unsettle social conventions of subjectivity. From Lucier's "I am sitting in a room" to Acconci's "Seeebed" speech reveals an alternative view of presence. [Author Abstract]

23.)   **Lauf, C.**
Joseph Beuys: The pedagogue as persona.
Ph.D. dissertation, Columbia University. 1992.

This dissertation discusses the teaching practice of German artist Joseph Beuys (1921-86). It proceeds from the point of view that in order to understand the phenomenon that transformed Beuys from a sculptor of local stature to an artist with a world message and international renown, it is essential to look at the conditions that shaped him. I begin by sketching the historical context of the German postwar period during which Beuys was educated. This is accomplished by an analysis of the pedagogy of Beuys's teacher, Ewald Matare (1886-1965). I posit that the fairly conservative artistic training Beuys received in bronze and stone sculpture formed his artistic outlook until external conditions--the arrival of Fluxus in Dusseldorf in 1962--mitigated otherwise. Upon the advent of Fluxus, Beuys radically altered his way of working from a sculptural and drawing style employing largely natural imagery to an adaptation of performance techniques, in tandem with found objects that constituted the vocabulary of Fluxus artists such as George Brecht, Nam June Paik, and Wolf Vostell. More important than the change in Beuys's formal style, however, was his new conviction that art could bear a social message. This message, according to Beuys, was that "everyone is an artist." In order to implement his idea, as well as a host of supporting notions encompassing cultural and political concepts, Beuys crafted a charismatic artistic persona that infused his work with mystical overtones and led him to be called "shaman" and "messianic" in the popular press. Beuys's ability to weld his personal appearance with his work and his performances was an art of rhetoric. He wielded such power as a professor at the Dusseldorf Academy of Art that by 1970, his classes numbered in the hundreds. With the aid of documents from an archive in the Resource Collection of the Getty Center for the History of the Arts and Humanities, I have attempted to reconstruct the conditions that finally made Beuys's pedagogy impossible at the Academy. I conclude with an overview of Beuys's legacy to contemporary artists, the third generation. In the appendices, a series of interviews with Fluxus artists, the former Director of the Kunstakademie, and Beuys's colleagues, provides primary source material that rounds out my vision of Beuys as pedagogue. A comprehensive bibliography with this focus in mind is also included. [Author Abstract]

24.)   **Lee, Y.**
The origins of video art.
D.Phil. dissertation, University of Oxford (United Kingdom). 1998.

This thesis is to examine the origins and development of video as an art form. It covers the ten-year period from the beginnings of the art in 1963 to the formation of its different genres in the mid-1970s.It studies the historical and environmental background against which video art emerged, the early video artists, landmark exhibitions, and the genres and unique characteristics of the video medium and video art. The historical and environmental background is studied in three stages. The first centers around the change in the media environment resulting from the development and use of video technology to challenge television. The second focuses on the relationship between early video art and Fluxus, whose members contributed to its birth. The third deals with the counter-culture of the 1960s, which influenced video art, both politically and formally. The thesis sheds light on the activities of the Fluxus members - Nam June Paik, Wolf Vostell and George Brecht - who set out a template for video art prior to the advent of the video medium itself, and also on work by artists who became active in the art in Europe and the United States after the video camera came on the scene. As for historic exhibitions of video art, the thesis reviews the TV as a Creative Medium show held at the Howard Wise Gallery in 1969 and other major shows organised in the United States, Germany, England, France and the Netherlands since late 1960s.As regards genres, this thesis approaches video art under the main headings of documentary, performance video, image processing, video installations and sculpture and feminist video. Video, because of its characteristics as a medium, is a tool for reproduction and realism. Although video art is an independent art quite different from television or film, its identity has yet to be established. The autonomy of video and the future of video culture are also studied. [Author Abstract]

25.) **Lim, S.**
Intermedial art and cybernetic vision: Nam June Paik in Germany, 1956-63.
Ph.D. dissertation, Lancaster University (United Kingdom). 2010.

This study traces Nam June Paik's intermedial art and cybernetic vision in his German period (1956-63) from the diverse activities as an Action Musician to the making of electronic media artwork. Most of the information was gathered from Paik's writings, correspondence and interviews. Much literature of Paik extols the new possibilities offered by Video Art, but Paik's early days in Germany, and his intermedial practice and cybernetic strategy of the period have been little explored. This study attempts to examine Paik's German period based on the concepts of intermedia and Cybernetics. Part I (chapters 1-3) provides the historical and conceptual background of Paik's art. It explains how Paik's avant-garde spirit began during his childhood; and it shows, in turn, how it had been developed to his dissertation on Arnold Schönberg in post-war Japan. Part I then focuses on the post-war techno-cultural discourses as tools for Paik's understanding of the relationship between electronic technology and human sensory perception before examining the art historical context of Paik's art through such avant-garde practices as Richard Wagner's Gesamtkunstwerk, John Cage's Experimental Music, the Darmstadt School and Fluxus. Part II (chapters 4-6) analyses Paik's artistic activities in Germany from a view of intermedia and Cybernetics. It is intended to contribute to an interdisciplinary project of mapping the early history of Nam June Paik's art. It argues that Paik German period represented an aesthetical moment in which the intermedial communication between body, language and technology were being reconfigured, and it suggests that Cybernetics played a significant role in framing Paik's ideas about complexity, interactivity, and participative creative around this shifting technological landscape. [Author Abstract]

26.)   **McCann, J.**
Walter De Maria: The Lightning Field.
Ph.D. dissertation, University of Portsmouth (United Kingdom). 2009.

Both De Maria and The Lightning Field have largely been critiqued solely with the art-historical framework of "Land Art" This thesis argues that such a framework has been too homogeneous and too narrow in its scope to do justice to the true complexities either of the artist's practice or of the visitor's experience of The Lightning Field, which involves considerably more than the dramatic spectacle of lightning. It proposes that De Maria's wide-ranging artistic career during the 1960's in Minimalism and in Happenings, in proto-Fluxus and as a musician provides a crucial context for an understanding of The Lightning Field. It argues that De Maria's engagement in music is of far greater significance than so far recognised, and that an exploration of the work of experimental composers John Cage, La Monte Young, and Steve Reich facilitates a richer understanding of many aspects of the visitor's experience of The Lightning Field. The thesis reviews the literature on "Land Art" before going on to provide a much more detailed account of De Maria's career in music as well as in art prior to the making of The Lightning Field, in order to give some flavour of the true breadth of his interest and friendships.   It also provides a thorough reassessment of what has mistakenly been construed as De Maria's critical silence. After giving brief details of The Lightning Field's construction and visiting arrangements, the next four chapters explore a number of hitherto neglected aspects of the visitor's experience of the work "driving, walking, watching, slowing down, listening, imagining" especially in relation to spatiotemporal concerns in experimental music. De Maria's aesthetic has been remarkably consistent throughout his career, despite the variety of means used to explore it, and the concluding chapter examines some of De Maria's more recent works in order to demonstrate his continuing concern for the complex dynamic between art, audience, and environment. [Author Abstract]

27.) McFadden, J. P.
Practices of site: Walter de Maria and Robert Morris, 1960--1977.
Ph.D. dissertation, The University of Texas at Austin. 2004.

This dissertation is a history of site-related practice in the work of Robert Morris and Walter de Maria. Grounded in a close analysis of the spatio-temporal conditions of their work from the early 1960s forward, this study investigates site as an important epistemological condition of this time. In pairing these two artists, who have associations with the art historical categories of Fluxus, Minimalism, Land Art, Conceptual Art, and Installation, this study also reconsiders the limitations of these categories. This study is arranged in roughly chronological form and considers a variety of experiential models in relationship to site. Chapter One addresses the early interdisciplinary and performative practices of the two artists in association with the emergence of Fluxus, new dance, and minimal music. Chapter Two considers how the diverse intermedia conditions of the early 1960s affect an understanding of minimalism in the work of De Maria and Morris. Chapter Three investigates the two well-known extensive site-related works of Morris and De Maria--De Maria's The Lightning Field (1971-1977), and Morris' Observatory (1971/1977). Chapter Four explores the print media as a site of practice for these artists during this period. [Author Abstract]

28.) **Medina-González, C.**
Fluxus non-art and anti-art: a study of George Maciunas.
Ph.D. dissertation, University of Essex (United Kingdom). 2003.

A reconstruction of the anti-artistic project of George Maciunas (1931-1978), the leader of the Fluxus movement. It follows the development of Maciunas's thoughts and activities, from the inception of his "concretist" theories at the time he was an art history student in New York in the late 1950s, and through the development of Fluxus in Europe and the United States. The dissertation covers in detail the different polemics and conflicts within the Fluxus group, in particular the widening of Maciunas's intellectual differences with the practitioners of the Happening, up to the rise of Maciunas's theory of "Fluxamusement" in 1965-1966. Apart of many other obscure points in the history of the group, the dissertation tries to elucidate the political rationale of Fluxus anti-art, under the light of the history and discourses of the Cold War. It explores in particular the relationship between Maciunas's pursuit of an aesthetics of efficiency and the economic contest between the superpowers. It explains the radicalisation of Maciunas's and Henry Flynt's campaign against art of 1963-1965 in relation to the shift of cultural discourses in the Soviet Union during the last period of the Khruschev era. On that basis, the dissertation develops a reading of the notion of "anti-art" as a systematic opposition to the notions of artistic autonomy and aesthetic semblance. It explores Maciunas's understanding of fine art and that of classical Kantian aesthetics, so as to describe Fluxus tension and complicity with the discourses of production in modernity, particularly under Soviet socialism. Finally, the dissertation offers a reading of Fluxus humour both in relation to the history of the ideas about purgation and the tensions between the physical and the intellectual in modern culture. [Author Abstract]

29.)   **Mesch, U. C.**
Problems of remembrance in postwar German performance art.
Ph.D. dissertation, The University of Chicago. 1997.

In this dissertation I examine the work of Wolf Vostell and Joseph Beuys, two artists working in West Germany after 1960, and consider the ways in which each artist deployed performance art to explore the dynamics of individual and collective memory. In a departure from the practices of John Cage, Fluxus, and the concerns of Concrete Art in the Rheinland in the early 1960s, Vostell and Beuys developed a particularly embodied and synesthetic experience of performance. These strategies were to retrieve collective experience and the capacity to remember as a means of resisting the atomizing coordination of desire by the mass media in Reconstruction Germany. I outline the Frankfurt School's revision and critique of Henri Bergson's theory of memory within the model of an emancipatory notion of remembrance developed by Max Horkheimer, Walter Benjamin, Herbert Marcuse, and Jurgen Habermas. This understanding of memory comprised the intellectual context for the development of performance in West Germany in the 1960s. I describe Vostell's performances in public space of the 1960s, in which the German postwar city becomes an allegorical "mnemotechnic" space for remembering technological destruction. I then argue that two major impulses characterize Beuys' action-performances. In the '60s, Beuys enacted autobiographical memory as a means of accessing collective memory of the recent past, and as a link to his theory of art as social sculpture. Beuys later institutionalized his theory of social sculpture in the organizations of the Office for Direct Democracy and the Free International University in realizing a public sphere within an existing art institution in his Documenta installations of the '70s. I examine how Beuys' work of the '70s engages and expands the institutional strategies of conceptual art. Finally I discuss Beuys' most ambitious enactment of social sculpture in his activities within the eco-activist Grunen and in his candidacy for the German parliament. While Beuys' infiltration of party politics ended with his withdrawal from conventional politics in 1983, his engagement with the Greens, which absorbed other spheres of life into the realm of art, almost realized his totalizing and mnemonic notion of art. [Author Abstract]

30.)   **Mount, A. L.**
Participatory art practice: What does it mean to participate?
Ed.D. dissertation, Teachers College, Columbia University. 2011.

Currently there is a growing volume of literature published about participation in art. The vast majority of that literature is art historical, and is concerned with identifying or clarifying participation. Much of this literature therefore merely documents this presence. It does not question either the recurrent characteristic of participation, as I assert throughout this dissertation. Nor do these art historical documents question the current resilience of participation--from the late 90's through to today, a developing discussion about participation, and the use of participation in art has been strongly in evidence. This is exactly where I would position the research presented in this dissertation. In order to do this properly, I have investigated some of the history of participation, but not to attempt to locate any one way of working or method as the definition of participation. Rather, I am more interested in connecting three stages--which I call crystallizations of art throughout the 20 th century: Dada and Brecht up to the 1930's, Fluxus and Beuys through the 1960's, and the growing number of artists involved in participation in art from the 1990's to today. I specifically address how the most progressive art of these eras involved participation in one way or another. Therefore, in writing this research, I have attempted to maintain focus upon the notion of the persistence of participation throughout several decades of art production. I have constructed a study of participation that conveys to the reader what participation has allowed this or that artist to achieve, raising the question: what are the effects of the work? But ultimately, throughout this engagement with art history, I wanted to discover what the differences might be between the forms of participation present today, and those of the Fluxus era, and those within the earlier Dada artworks. Throughout the study I use Joseph Beuys, Bertolt Brecht and Ivan Illich as constant sources of historical reference along with several others. The study analyses and compares the work of Superflex, Anton Vidokle and Tino Sehgal in order to establish a range of forms of participation in art today, and establish its interconnectivity to historical precedents along with philosophical and art historical theory. The study compares the positions of Jacques Rancière, Chantal Mouffe as continual guides, and the work of noted art historians and critics such as Umberto Eco, Claire Bishop and Nicolas Bourriaud. Their work, along with many others is used to tease out of the concepts of participation both similarities over decades and validity in the claims of the artists to generate a sense of the meaning of participation as a form and as art. [Author Abstract]

31.) **Munroe, A.**
Avant-garde art in postwar Japan: The culture and politics of radical critique, 1951-
-1970.
Ph.D. dissertation, New York University. 2004.

This dissertation of avant-garde art in postwar Japan is based upon a previous publication by the author titled Japanese Art After 1945: Scream Against the Sky (New York: Harry N. Abrams, 1994). Focusing on key art movements and artists' groups which defined postwar discourses on radical critique, this history charts the intellectual, aesthetic, and stylistic developments of avant-garde art in Japan from circa 1951 to 1970, a period defined by the leftist struggle against the renewal of the U.S.-Japan Security Treaty, known as Anpo. Both American and Japanese historians have studied the sociopolitical debates that mark the postwar period. What is less well-known is the history of new artistic forms and practices that emerged from this era of unprecedented upheaval, and how radical artists' strategies underscored and reworked the leftist discourses on democratic revolution, political subjectivity, and cultural anarchism. This study examines the avant-garde within the broader context of postwar Japanese social, political, and cultural history, focusing on its vigorous critique of the ruling ideologies of modernization and its opposition to institutionalized culture and politics. This dissertation originated as an art historical research topic and certain formalist modes of stylistic analysis and aesthetic interpretation prevail. Among the questions explored here are: How can national characteristics of modern art be defined within a global discourse of modernity and modernism? If originality is the crux of the modernist adventure, how do we interpret this work within the framework of the modernist discourse? Drawing on extensive primary sources and interviews, this dissertation aims to construct the first history in English of the following art movements: Gutai Art Association, Bokujin-kai and Sodeisha, the Yomiuri Indépendant's Anti-Art groups, Obsessional Art and Ankoku Butoh dance, VIVO and the Postwar School of Photography, Tokyo Fluxus and Conceptual Art, and the Mono-ha movement. The Introduction describes the Anpo movement, whose periodization defines this study; reviews the Taisho and Showa prehistory of the Japanese avant-garde; explores the discourse on cultural autonomy in modern Japanese intellectual debates; and offers a theoretical framework for defining the terminology of "radical critique." The Conclusion reviews the contradictions inherent in the Japanese avant-garde's embrace of leftist cultural critiques, and identifies problematic issues of historicizing zen'ei (avant-garde) and gendai (contemporary) art. [Author Abstract]

32.)   **Nettleton, T. E. F.**
Throw Out the Books, Get Out in the Streets: Subjectivity and Space in Japanese Underground Art of the 1960s.
Ph.D. dissertation, University of Rochester. 2011.

This dissertation examines the relationship between subjectivity and spatialization, or the dynamic process of understanding space in terms of social and psychic relations, as it is articulated in the works of Japanese avant-garde and underground artists of the politically turbulent decade of the 1960s. The premise of this work is that analyses of social spaces and subjectivity are necessary to adequately understand the period's Japanese avant-garde and underground art practices. It takes up this task by scrutinizing, in addition to the actual works, their documentation, and critical and popular receptions, academic and popular print media of the era in order to situate them in their specific cultural context. I examine a broad range of artists to reflect the dense connection between artists of the 1960s who were working with different media. The artists include Fluxus-affiliated art collective Hi Red Center; Yoko Ono, who was an important figure for not only her own groundbreaking work but also her introduction of happenings and events to Japanese audiences; dramatist, essayist, filmmaker, and poet Shuji Terayama; acclaimed experimental filmmaker and a trenchant critic Toshio Matsumoto; and preeminent "Shochiku Nouvelle Vague" director and left-wing polemicist Nagisa Oshima. While the content and medium of their works vary, they all address the complex relation between subjects and the urban environment and offer critical responses to the larger postwar cultural and political climates, which were shaped significantly by Japan's relation to the U.S. The works I consider suggest that this relation also took on cultural, psychic, and sexual dimensions. I conclude that by focusing on the performance of socially inscribed bodies in the urban environment, these artists show, against the myth of Japanese homogeneity, that space and subjectivity are products of social relations, always marked by class, gender, racial and sexual difference. [Author Abstract]

33.) **O'Neill, R.**
Ecole de Nice, 1956--1971.
Ph.D. dissertation, City University of New York. 2003.

The Ecole de Nice of the 1960s has been broadly defined to include artists associated with three distinct artistic tendencies--Nouveau Réalisme, Fluxus, and Supports/Surfaces. The focus of this study is the five most significant artists of the Ecole de Nice--Yves Klein, Arman, Martial Raysse, Ben Vautier, and Claude Viallat. Despite their stylistic diversity and affiliations, the conceptual affinities shared by these artists and their sense of cultural autonomy have not been examined. Consequently, the Ecole de Nice, though given some credibility as the result of museum exhibitions, has largely remained ill-defined and historically neglected. This dissertation will demonstrate that the Ecole de Nice is an important historical phenomenon inseparable from the Riviera, but also a gauge of the broader changes impacting France in the 1960s. Even more so than Paris, the Ecole de Nice called attention to the implications of Americanization (consumerism, mass culture, and tourism), and they epitomized the national emphasis on rejuvenation associated with a younger demographic, and the Mediterranean region. Beyond direct or metaphoric reference to the locale, all five artists created a visual language meant to engage the public with the experience of their new reality by predicating their work on direct perception and sensations, and rejecting intellectualization and introverted subjectivity. All five artists devised theatrical modes of presentation based on the strategy of appropriation and the use of readymade objects and spaces to counter the dominance of painting as a vehicle of formalist innovation, the basis of the Ecole de Paris. The Ecole de Nice promoted artistic pluralism. These artists drew from the array of modernist trends, but this study will emphasize the clear links these artists made to the classical and modern traditions associated with the Riviera, and the new reality of consumerism and tourism, which characterized the region's postwar development. I suggest that the emergence of the Ecole de Nice internally eroded the dominance of Parisian culture as the national standard, and provided a new model of French pluralism that remains distinct yet comparable to international trends of the 1960s. [Author Abstract]

34.) **Otty, L.**
Signals and noise: art, literature and the avant-garde.
Ph.D. dissertation, The University of Edinburgh (United Kingdom). 2009.

Avant-gardes such as Expressionism, Dada, Surrealism, Futurism, Fluxus and Pop were composed not only of painters but also dramatists, musicians, actors, singers, dancers, sculptors, poets and architects. Their works represent a dramatic process of crossfertilization between the arts, resulting in an array of hybrid forms that defy conventional categorisation. This thesis investigates implications of this cross-disciplinary impulse and aims by doing so to open out a site in which to reassess both the manner in which the avant-gardes have been theorised and the impact their theorisation has had on contemporary aesthetics. In the first part, I revisit the work of the most influential theorists of the avant-garde in order to ask what the term "avant-garde" has come to signify. I look at how different theories of the avant-garde and of modernism relate to one another. The work of Theodor Adorno provides a connective tissue throughout the thesis. In Chapter One, I use it to complicate Peter Bürger's notion of the avant-garde as "anti-art" and to argue that the most pressing challenge that the avant-gardes announce is to think through the cross-disciplinarity that marks their work. In Chapter Two, I trace how painting has come to be considered as the paradigmatic modernist art form and how, as a result, the avant-garde has been read as a secondary, "literary" phenomenon to be grasped through its relation to painting. I argue this constitutes a systematic devaluation of literature and has resulted in an "art historical" model of the avant-gardes which represses both their real radicality and implications of their work for these kinds of disciplinary structures. In the second part, I explore works which examine and question the aesthetic hierarchies and notions of aesthetic autonomy that the theories of modernism and the avant-garde explored in the first part set up. In Chapter Three, I approach by way of two cross-disciplinary works which employ literature and visual art: Marcel Duchamp's *Green Box* (1934) and Andy Warhol's A; *a novel* (1968). Works such as these, which slip through the gaps between literary and art history, have, I argue, important implications for literary and visual aesthetics but are often overlooked in disciplinary histories. In my final chapter, I return to the theory of the avant-garde as it emerges in the work of Jean-Francois Lyotard. I examine how his work reconfigures Adorno's aesthetics by performing the cross-disciplinary movement that it argues is characteristic of avant-garde art works. Tracing his "post-aesthetic" response to Duchamp and Warhol, I explore how Lyotard articulates a mode of practice that moves beyond the dichotomy of "art" and "antiart" and opens out a site in which the importance of the twentieth century avant-gardes is made visible. [Author Abstract]

35.)   **Patton, R. M.**

Games as artistic medium: Interfacing complexity theory in game-based art pedagogy.

Ph.D. dissertation, The Pennsylvania State University. 2011.

Having computer skills, let alone access to a personal computer, has become a necessary component of contemporary Western society and many parts of the world. Digital media literacy involves youth being able to view, participate in, and make creative works with technologies in personal and meaningful ways. Games, defined in this study as structured play, provided the foundation for many of the works from 20th century art movements, such as Dadaism, Surrealism, Situationism, and Fluxus. I argue that these artists used games as methods to explore and expose rules and systems in ways of understanding the world through art. I describe how these artworks embodied complexity thinking in their use of game making methods to expose social, political, economic, and environmental systems. The game-based art pedagogy derived from this art history, also draws from the features of game-like unit operations (Bogost, 2006), strategies and tactics (de Certeau, 1997), and infinite play (Carse, 1987) to foster a critical aesthetic. Complexity thinking (or complexity theory), represents a way for constructing meaning that involves the integration of multiple types of systems, including dynamic models, closed-looped systems, and the ability to transfer one model of a system to another situation or phenomenon. Emergent behavior is supported in the complex systems modeled in video games such as SimCity and Civilization. Much of game-based art pedagogy research centers on students learning by playing games. Learning history or other factual data in the form of games has value, however using games in this way does not encapsulate games as an artistic medium for creative purposes, only as a means for teaching. That is, while students created video games in a variety of classroom environments over the last fifteen years, typically it was done to learn subjects like math, computer science, or to develop language skills. In my action research study, I began with the premise based on my prior teaching experience, that video game creation was an attainable goal by youth, and a valuable studio project in the art classroom to understand complexity in social systems, and learn an art history of games as artworks. I recruited youth (ages of 8-13) and taught them how to make games in four iterations of a game creation course. The make-up of the courses comprised one class of middle school girls, two classes of elementary school children, and one class of middle school boys and girls. Each class met during a five-day course, learning concepts and methods of game development by playing and making physical, board, and video games. New curricular elements for the research included a physical game activity, a mobile game using 2-D barcodes, a tabletop game connecting the video game instruction, and game cards written as independent programmable unit operations. Students made video games that used the concepts of move, avoid, release, and contact (MARC) as a method I designed for exploring complexity thinking. I observed and recorded the participants' game making process; collected their games, journals, and pre and post surveys; and from these observations and feedback, I reviewed and revised the curriculum for each class. I interviewed the other course instructors who used the curriculum that I developed providing additional insight to the pedagogy, delivery of the curriculum, and student learning. Three months after the courses ended, a sample set of students and parents took part in follow-up interviews regarding the impact of the course. Because games, specifically digital games (also called video games), are seen as potentially corrupting to children, I gathered parental input on their child's involvement. At the center of this study's curriculum, playful, game-like methods were used to create game-based artworks. Students critiqued games using detailed, expressive language to describe how games work, critically aware of how commercial games differ in complexity. From their game making experiences, students gained confidence and knowledge finding game structures in everyday life and how to make programmable media like video games. This study argues that learning through game-based art pedagogy, students begin to understand complexity thinking by producing digital media as a form of artistic expression, and as a form of preparation for future learning in and beyond a 4-12th grade art curriculum. [Author Abstract]

36.) **Perkins, S. E.**
Artists' periodicals and alternative artists' networks: 1963--1977.
Ph.D. dissertation, The University of Iowa. 2003.

Periodicals published by the historic avant-garde are key elements in these group's strategies for cultural empowerment. This often neglected area of art historical inquiry constitutes a continuous genre from the beginnings of the twentieth century to the present day. I argue that up to World War II these periodicals are concerned almost exclusively with refuting and advancing new cultural texts, accompanied by a re-examination of the typographic conventions, space and materiality of the traditional printed page. My central area of investigation is bracketed by two key post-World War II periodicals. The first is the pre-Fluxus periodical An Anthology (1963) and I conclude with the initiation of the correspondence art periodical Commonpress (1977-1990). Both periodicals are examples of the new genre of "artists' periodicals" and they mark the shift from the periodical as a site for the reproduction of texts, to one in which artist and reader collaborate in the production of new texts and experiences. The periodicals published by Fluxus serve as the armature through which I examine the transformation of the periodical within the expanded arts activities of the alternative arts milieu of the 1960s. I claim that Fluxus' periodicals lie at the heart of its constitution as a community and were instrumental in constructing Fluxus as an imagined "conceptual country." The final series of periodicals that I examine all play defining roles in the emergence and consolidation of the international correspondence art network (aka., mail art and the Eternal Network). Network periodicals played a pivotal role in establishing this alternative communications network. Particular attention is paid to a new genre of periodicals, assembling magazines that develop and sustain this anti-hierarchical network. I claim that Commonpress' existence was only possible through the consolidation of this self-sustaining communications network. Common to all the periodicals examined is the perennial avant-garde quest to dissolve the boundaries between art and life. This anti-formalist and utopian history is revealed as the larger text which activated these often overlooked, but vital arenas of post-World War II avant-garde activity. [Author Abstract]

37.) **Pisaro, K. G.**
Music from scratch: Cornelius Cardew, experimental music and the Scratch Orchestra in Britain in the 1960s and 1970s.
Ph.D. dissertation, Northwestern University. 2001.

This dissertation examines the Scratch Orchestra, an experimental music organization founded in 1969 in London by Cornelius Cardew with Michael Parsons and Howard Skempton, ending in 1974. Providing a detailed record and analysis of the orchestra's music and activities, it uses interview data collected by the author from over twenty former orchestra members, personal letters, orchestral archival material, newsletters and previously unreleased musical scores as well as musicological, ethnomusicological and sociological analytical and research tools and resources. The Scratch Orchestra, described by Cardew in the article "A Scratch Orchestra: draft constitution" (Musical Times, June 1969), combined social, musical and political ideals. The orchestra, totaling over 100 members, included well-known musicians such as John Tilbury, Brian Eno, Michael Nyman, John White and visual artists, students, scientists and lawyers, some with little to no formal musical training. Politically the group sought to effect social change through an all-encompassing view of music, first by incorporating an expansive view of composition, sounds, locations and audiences and later through a direct application of Communist political philosophy. This document begins tracing the roots of the orchestra through the influence of John Cage, MEV, Fluxus, AMM and the Portsmouth Sinfonia. The next major section, the history of the Scratch Orchestra, describes not only activities and situations but delineates the inextricable relationship between social, musical and political ideals and activities beginning in the early, "honeymoon" phase and continuing through the political change and the end. The dissertation's second half categorizes and analyzes the music through its relationship to Cardew's repertory categories in the Draft Constitution. Music on Scratch Orchestra concerts included the new genres of Scratch Music (notated accompaniments of indefinite length) and Improvisation Rites (simple structures creating community in improvisation), performances of major works by Cornelius Cardew (i) and Christian Wolff (Burdocks), as well as orchestra members' compositions, the orchestra's unique interpretation of popular classics and extensive multiple media presentations. Appendices include a list of members and concerts, and catalogs of the Scratch Orchestra archive and the British Library's Cardew Collection. [Author Abstract]

38.) Remeselnik, J.
Motion(less) pictures: The cinema of stasis.
Ph.D. dissertation, Wayne State University. 2012.

Since cinema's inception, there has been much disagreement among film theorists about the role of movement in cinema's ontology. For example, while Rudolf Arnheim has argued that motion is a sine qua non of cinema, Roland Barthes has insisted that motion is not as central to cinema's ontology as duration, an experiential "unfolding." In this dissertation, I argue--following Barthes--that movement is merely a contingent, not a necessary, condition of cinema. I further suggest that the very enterprise of prescribing necessary conditions of cinema is myopic, reductive, and reactionary. In supporting these claims, I interrogate the cinema of stasis, a modality of avant-garde films which feature little or no movement. By foregrounding stillness, these films often blur the lines between cinema and other art forms, including photography, painting, and literature. Giving especially close attention to films by Andy Warhol, Fluxus, Michael Snow, and Derek Jarman, I explore the aesthetic and affective valences of cinematic stasis, while drawing attention to the numerous ways that static films broaden our conception of what films can be and do. [Author Abstract]

39.)   **Rhee, J.**
Performing the other: Asian bodies in performance and video art, 1950s--1990s.
Ph.D. dissertation, Boston University. 2002.

This dissertation examines the shifting identities of Asian diasporal artists by examining Nam June Paik and Yoko Ono in local and global contexts. As Asians who received Western educations and deeply involved themselves in the international art world, each of these artists confronted the problem of defining themselves in regard to cultures that often viewed them within an ethnic or "native" frame. While these artists drew on their respective Asian traditions, the postwar Western avant-garde played a major role in shaping their work. By delving into the reception of their works both in the West and in their countries of origin, I argue that their particular "border" positions created an interface between the rigid dichotomy of East and West. Investigating the cultural and historical contexts for their performances and videos in Europe, the U.S., and Asia, this dissertation demonstrates that the Asian body reads differently according to its staging. Chapter One introduces this theme by examining how the notion of Asia was itself constructed and how that construction shifted after World War II. Chapters Two, Three and Four present Paik and Ono, who began their artistic careers in the 1960s' art movement Fluxus. Despite their important roles in establishing Fluxus as international, their participation was constantly framed within their native cultures, often under the rubric of Zen Buddhism. In their native countries, on the other hand, these artists were presented as

Western, thus essentially foreign to their cultural traditions. While their otherness gained much attention from Western viewers, the advantage of being "exotic" also limited the meanings to be found in their art. In the 1990s, postmodern artists often positioned themselves as multinational. The conclusion presents this new generation with Mariko Mori, who employs pastiches of East and West, past and future in her video art. By investigating the social, cultural, and personal aspects in these Asian diasporal artists' art, this dissertation addresses how that art produced a liberating interface between East and West that went beyond Orientalism during the postwar period. [Author Abstract]

40.)   **Robinson, J. E.**
From abstraction to model: In the event of George Brecht & the conceptual turn in the art of the 1960s.
Ph.D. dissertation, Princeton University. 2008.

This dissertation explores George Brecht's model of the event score as part of the shift in artistic practice away from abstract painting toward conceptual propositions, situating that turn at the beginning of the 1960s. If Jackson Pollock was the first major influence on Brecht and his generation, John Cage and Robert Rauschenberg quickly emerged to take his place toward the end of the 1950s. At the same time, the work of Marcel Duchamp was becoming increasingly visible in New York, inspiring new uses of everyday objects in the context of art. Attending to all of these significant influences, the dissertation provides the first detailed study of Brecht's development of the event score. Brecht studied Experimental Composition with Cage at The New School for Social Research in New York in 1958 and 1959, and learnt the structure of the score, which would prove a resilient conceptual matrix, able to contain aspects of perception beyond the aural. At the time, Brecht was pondering the use of found objects in his art, which he set in relation to textual instructions and prompts. He attempted to "score" those objects, to cue each new subject's capacities for abstracting thought from what is given. In tandem with his extension of the Cagean score model, Brecht developed his concept of abstraction, as a process one could envisage, in relation to the philosophy of Ernst Cassirer, which he also studied at the New School in this period. With his concept of "events," Brecht was addressing a prevailing sense among artists of the static qualities of painting. As critics were facing difficulties characterizing the dramatic example of Pollock's radically active approach to painting, the force of language began to shift, away from the discursive field surrounding the work of art, into the hands of artists. This migration of the function of language is an important subtext of the dissertation. In was in this context that Brecht's event score, presented as text, aimed to cue perception, and extend creative process beyond the artist, to the subject. As late as 1957, Duchamp formally presented his thesis on "The Creative Act," which stressed the significant gap between an artist's intentions and what is realized in the form of the work, including the famous adage that it is the spectator who completes the work. "The Creative Act" was reproduced in the important Robert Lebel monograph of 1959, and, as Brecht recognized, it dovetailed with the indeterminacy at the heart of Cage's approach to composition. The theses of Duchamp and Cage are an implicit aspect of Brecht's events. Writing his first short score, Time-Table Music, in 1959, Brecht gradually moved beyond music. By 1961 he had arrived at the form of the event score. In their resolved form, Brecht's event scores could be realized as an object, a performance, or simply as an idea. The dissertation explores the Fluxus context in which Brecht's scores have been most known, while also attempting to insert them into wider frameworks, from which Brecht has remained conspicuously absent. First, it sets Brecht's early work in relation to that of Rauschenberg and Jasper Johns, considering Duchamp reception, the use of everyday objects and modes of participation. And finally Brecht's event scores are reinserted into the context of the formal and linguistic cues to perception developed almost contemporaneously in Minimalism and Conceptual Art. [Author Abstract]

41.)   **Rodenbeck, J. F.**
Crash: Happenings (as) the black box of experience, 1958--1966.
Ph.D. dissertation, Columbia University. 2003.

Crash: a disaster of machinic impact; a singular and accidental event, unrepeatable. The very name of Jim Dine's 1960 happening "Car Crash" points symptomatically to an "accidental" violence that pervaded the performance works known as happenings: the time-stoppage of disaster, which organizes the event not towards some positive construction of presence but radically, negatively towards absence. In the late 1950's a number of New York-based visual artists--including Allan Kaprow, Claes Oldenburg, Jim Dine, and artists associated with Fluxus, NO Art, Neo-dada and (later) Pop--began to produce event-structures. "Happening," the name Kaprow selected to designate this new time-based art, was an intentionally vague term chosen to avoid association with the theater and to conjure less textual, more popular cognates. In part as a result of what was in effect a terminological disarticulation, the happenings have never been adequately dealt with either historically or formally; they have served instead as curious addenda to the history of the early 1960s, inhabiting the problematic liminal space--between painting and theater, between art and life--formulated by Kaprow. The accident--which negates both object and durational structure-- haunts happenings and has rendered them marginal, if not irrecuperable, to the official histories of post-war art. This dissertation attempts a partial recovery of that negation--and its history--by examining the relations between happenings and two kinds of reproduction: theater and photography. The critical aporia is addressed in three ways. First, I examine happenings as "second generation" post-war artifacts; second, I assess the latent content described by the category itself; and third, I analyze salient features of canonical works--particularly of their material, formal and thematic structure--and proposes a set of readings which places the happenings in complex relation to contemporaneous artistic practices. [Author Abstract]

42.) **Sammons, L. L.**
Audience Interactivity and the Concert Hall Audience.
Ph.D. dissertation, University of Virginia. 2012.

The second half of the 20th century and the beginning of the 21st have witnessed the creation of a largely unanalyzed body of works that harness as a creative force audiences gathered together for a shared musical experience. This dissertation seeks to examine the emergence of these audience-interactive works, offer classification designed to illustrate the range of such works, consider the myriad aesthetic and social concerns that composers of these works must address, and contribute to this oeuvre through the composition of new audience-interactive works. This dissertation explores audience interactive music and its creation through concepts like Christopher Small's "musicking" and Nicolas Bourriaud's "relational aesthetics" and situates audience interactivity within work from scholars of play, ethnomusicology, and aesthetics. The dissertation also includes in-depth analysis of audience-interactive pieces composed by Pauline Oliveros, Robert Ashley, Jason Freeman, Bruce Adolphe, and members of Fluxus. The composition portion of the dissertation consists of five works: a set of event scores calling for audience improvisation, a work for computer-generated sound and images resulting from data produced by audience-directed sensors, a branching musical structure through which a performer navigates based on audience preferences, a system for reading characteristics of an audience as notation, and a piece in which audience members move about the performance space to offer individual musical prompts to performers. This collection of compositions demonstrates both the diversity of techniques for achieving audience interactivity and the multitude of purposes for which audience interactivity may be used. Taken as a whole, the dissertation aims to comprehensively consider concert-hall-audience-based audience interactivity through analytical, theoretical, and creative means. [Author Abstract]

43.) **Santone, J. L.**
Circulating the event: the social life of performance documentation, 1965--1975.
Ph.D. dissertation, McGill University (Canada). 2011.

This dissertation reevaluates the relationship between performance acts and documents by considering the way documentation was understood within the time of an event. Expanding on Alain Badiou's theory of evental 'Twoness' in Being and Event , I develop an approach to performance that always takes documents and performance acts together, as corresponding producers of an art event. Looking at acts and documents together, one notices how the type of repetition enacted between them allows for variation and novelty in an event. One important implication of this approach is a stronger valuation of audiences of performance, including audiences that may not have been present to witness a live event. I investigate several cases of private or unannounced conceptual performances from the late 1960s to make my argument here. In these performances - On Kawara's I got up (1968-79), Alison Knowles's The Identical Lunch (1968-73), Adrian Piper's Concrete Infinity Documentation Piece (1970), and Mieko Shiomi's Spatial Poem (1965-75) - the artists study everyday phenomena, drawing our attention to what is otherwise unnoticed and engaging participation by encouraging repetition. As documents of these serial performances circulate, they help locate and sustain audiences. In the circulation of performance acts and documents, there is the potential as well for developing performance community, which is evident in an analysis of Fluxus performances, like Spatial Poem. The events studied here, in different ways, reveal that even seemingly private performances are fundamentally social in their orientation. [Author Abstract]

44.) **Schrank, B.**
Play Beyond Flow: A Theory of Avant-garde Videogames.
Ph.D. dissertation, Georgia Institute of Technology. 2010.

Videogame tinkerers, players, and activists of the 21st century are continuing, yet redefining, the avant-garde art and literary movements of the 20th century. Videogames are diverging as a social, cultural, and digital medium. They are used as political instruments, artistic experiments, social catalysts, and personal means of expression. A diverse field of games and technocultural play, such as alternate reality games, griefer attacks, arcade sculptures, and so on, can be compared and contrasted to the avant-garde, such as contemporary tactical media, net art, video art, Fluxus, the Situationists, the work of Pollock or Brecht, Dada, or the Russian Formalists. For example, historical avant-garde painters played with perspectival space (and its traditions), rather than only within those grid-like spaces. This is similar in some ways to how game artists play with flow (and player expectations of it), rather than advancing flow as the popular and academic ideal. Videogames are not only an advanced product of technoculture, but are the space in which technoculture conventionalizes play. This makes them a fascinating site to unwork and rethink the protocols and rituals that rule technoculture. It is the audacity of imagining certain videogames as avant-garde (from the perspective of mainstream consumers and art academics alike) that makes them a good candidate for this critical experiment. [Author Abstract]

45.)   **Skurvidaite, S.**
States of self: Carolee Schneemann's works, 1962--1974.
Ph.D. dissertation, State University of New York at Stony Brook. 2006.

The dissertation comprises reconstructive narratives of Carolee Schneemann's seminal performative works of the 1960s and 1970s (primarily Eye/Body, 1962-63; Meat Joy, 1964; and Interior Scroll, 1974) situated in their specific art historical contexts, and analyses of these works from the psychoanalytic perspectives, including D.W.Winnicott's object relations theory, Paul Schilder's physio-psychological formation of the body image, and the behavioral and psychoanalytic theories that see art as a necessary disruption of order. Investigations of the alternative history of Performance Art lead to the early 20 th century avant-gardes, Futurism and Dada, transplanted via the Black Mountain College to the US, and renewed by the experimental artists' associations influenced by John Cage, primarily Happenings, Fluxus, and the Judson Dance Theater. The female erotic body as the origin of the self and as a social space-the premise of Schneemann's multivalent practice--aligns this study with historical, political and theoretical feminisms that inflect psychoanalytic methodologies in continuing discursive permutations. The aim of this dissertation is a comprehensive monographic study of the artist's works of the period in their historical and theoretical complexity. [Author Abstract]

46.) **Smith, L.**
Zen Buddhism and Mid-Century American Art.
M.A. thesis, State University of New York at Stony Brook. 2011.

This thesis is an explanation of the influence of the theoretical thought of Zen Buddhism on American art in the 1950s and 1960s. Zen Buddhism came to the United States through the efforts of Daisetz Teitaro Suzuki, a scholar on Buddhism, whose influence on artists and intellectuals of the 1950s led to an enormous amount of interest in the religion during that time. This influence led to a "Zen boom" and to a particular strain of Zen-inspired expression that the philosopher Alan Watts labeled "beat Zen." Composer John Cage took Zen ideas and converted them directly into a meditation on the moment: 4'33". Abstract painters such as Mark Tobey, Ad Reinhardt, and Robert Rauschenberg painted emptiness as an expression of the elimination of boundaries. In the 1960s Happenings and Fluxus emphasized the importance of direct experience and Korean-born artist Nam June Paik broke through the limits of duality by both a minimalistic and maximalistic means. In the end their importance lay in the unabashed desire to experience the world without filter and show that directness through their art. Although the art world moved into different areas by the late 1960s, away from unmediated experience of the world, their emphasis on this issue was the grounding of much of their work and was an expression of that particular time in art and culture. [Author Abstract]

47.)   Smith, O. F.
George Maciunas and a history of Fluxus; or, the art movement that never existed.
Ph.D. dissertation, University of Washington. 1991.

Fluxus is historically complex and philosophically difficult to define. This ambiguity, however, is an aspect of its radicality. Fluxus is both an attitude towards art making and culture that is not historically limited, and a specific historical group. As an attitude Fluxus is part of a larger conceptual development that is a significant, although often overlooked, current of the twentieth century Western avant-garde. Fluxus, though, was not a movement like Russian Constructivism or Surrealism. It was a fluid group of artists who were associated personally and conceptually at various times with the rubric "Fluxus." Fluxus was also an attitude based on an unpretentious directness that brought into question the notion of high art or, as they called it, "serious culture." The focus of this dissertation is the inter-relationship between Maciunas and Fluxus. It attempts to discern how the general developments of Fluxus were shaped by Maciunas' interactions with various artists and with the collective and individual projects of the group. Because of the central and unique roll Maciunas played in a history of the Fluxus Group, this study has been structured primarily around George Maciunas' activities in association with the whole of the Fluxus Group. This study is structured chronologically. Chapter one is a survey of related developments in twentieth century culture (related to the "second form of modernism") that had a generative influence on Fluxus. Chapters two through seven survey the historical development of the Fluxus Group, particularly as related to the organizational activities of George Maciunas. These historical activities can be broken into three broad, somewhat overlapping, chronological and conceptual stages: the proto-Fluxus period and the early period of Fluxus festivals and event performances from 1961-1964 (chapters two through five); the period of Fluxus publishing and multiples from 1964-1970 (Chapter six); the period of late Fluxus performances from 1970-1978 (Chapter seven). The last chapter (Chapter eight) is a consideration of the Fluxus attitude, the conceptual outlook that underlies the specific activities of the group. [Author Abstract]

48.)   **Sutton, G. H.**
The experience machine: Stan VanDerBeek's "Movie-Drome" and expanded cinema practices of the 1960s.
Ph.D. dissertation, University of California, Los Angeles. 2009.

The Experience Machine presents the first in-depth study of American artist Stan VanDerBeek (1927-1984), who was instrumental in the development of multimedia art during the postwar period. This dissertation analyzes how the perceptual conditions of his conceptual theater called Movie-Drome (1965) engendered an immersive subject by prioritizing multisensory experience over concerns exclusive to visual representation (mimesis or depiction). Movie-Drome was constituent of Expanded Cinema art works that employed several audio and visual projection sources and multiple screens in an intimate live performance environment. By creating an immersive experience that addressed a collective audience, Movie-Drome articulated a particular type of subjectivity for Expanded Cinema that broke from the singular modernist viewing subject of avant-garde film as well as the atomized mass audience associated with broadcast television. Rather than developing out of a genealogy of cinematic devices, Movie-Drome functioned as a communication tool, or in VanDerBeek's words, an "experience machine" and was situated in the center of the various radical aesthetic sensibilities that exploded in New York in the late 1950s and early 1960s including Fluxus, Happenings, Judson Church dance performances, and the minimal music of John Cage, who like VanDerBeek was part of the Land, an artist's colony in upstate New York. The thirty-one-foot-high metal dome structure VanDerBeek built on the Land was a prototype for a communications system in which several dromes would be positioned throughout the world, each linked to an orbiting satellite that would store and transmit images between the various sites. Movie-Drome's emphasis on two-way communication and data transfer introduced a telecommunications model for art production reflecting the larger transformation from a mechanical to information age. Through a close examination of Movie-Drome's formal traits and VanDerBeek's conceptual slides and drawings, this dissertation suggests that Expanded Cinema attempted to address broader political systems of distribution, social regulation, and the mechanization of information. Ultimately, The Experience Machine establishes a new interpretive framework for understanding multimedia art not as an accretion of film and computer technology, but as a critical means to engage the effects of mass media on the wider social and cultural experience of the late 1960s. [Author Abstract]

49.)   **Suzuki, D. P.**
Minimal music: Its evolution as seen in the works of Philip Glass, Steve Reich, Terry Riley, and La Monte Young.
Ph.D. dissertation, University of Southern California. 1991.

Philip Glass, Steve Reich, Terry Riley, and La Monte Young comprise a group of American composers who, in the 1960s, helped develop and advance a style of music known as Minimal music or Minimalism. Minimal music represents one of the most radical, distinctive, and significant stylistic developments of the twentieth century. Minimalism is a reductive approach to composition most often characterized by simple repetitive structures, restricted diatonic pitch materials, and a steady, unflagging pulse. It is also a style of music which was and remains controversial, though it has been embraced by many other composers. This dissertation traces the evolution of Minimal music and the aesthetics associated with it through the works of these four composers, as well as their involvement with the thriving arts community of the 1960s and early 1970s, primarily adherents of Fluxus, Minimal Art, and Conceptual Art. The development of the Minimalist style is also viewed through the advent of post-modern aesthetics which follow the works and ideas of John Cage, and the cultural milieu of the 1960s manifested through the influence of jazz, rock, and non-Western music. Each composer's compositional output is surveyed and analyzed, tracing the formation, establishment, and expansion of idiosyncratic compositional devices. The final chapter offers a survey of other Minimalist composers. [Author Abstract]

50.) **Tait, S.**

Becoming multiple: collaboration in contemporary art practice.

Ph.D. dissertation, Birmingham City University (United Kingdom). 2009.

This thesis begins with the question of whether a collaborative art practice inspired by, or drawing upon, Gilles Deleuze and Felix Guattari's concept of `the rhizome', and the notions of movement and change it implies, is possible within the structure required of doctoral study. The study is a vital contribution to the knowledge and understanding of contemporary collaborative art practice, with reference to more than half a dozen contemporary collaborative art groups, as well as The Situationist International, Zurich Dada and Fluxus, the thesis explores the composition and maintenance of collaborative practices. The study's art-practice-as-research has focused on the production of unexpected events or `glitches' and the problems of hierarchy and control where roles such as `collaborator' and `participant' come into contact. The relations in and between collaborative groups are considered in terms of what Deleuze and Guattari call `molarising' and `molecularising' forces, and the research included the discovery of new forms of what I have termed `Molecular collaboration'. The study seeks to address perceived weaknesses in certain (dominant) Marxist forms of critical/dialectical practice in relation to art by exploring alternative, more anarchist approaches to relations, roles and types of group organisation. The work of Manuel DeLanda on `assemblage theory' and Erving Goffman's concept of `role adjustments' are combined with Deleuze and Guattari's `diagrammatics' to develop the new concept of `Molecular collaboration' Molecular collaboration is an important concept because it frees collaborative working from the burden of individual and group identity by allowing creativity to be expressed immanently within a network of relations rather than in relation to any specific ideal or structure. [Author Abstract]

51.)   **Thorpe, J.**
Here hear: My recent compositions in a context of philosophy and Western 20th century experimental art.
M.A. thesis, York University (Canada). 2000.

This thesis consists of over two hours of music compositions that I have written since September 1999, as well as a paper providing philosophical and artistic context. It explains my philosophical interest in the art of Marcel Duchamp, John Cage, and Fluxus. A case is made for the philosophical and experiential equivalence of much of these artists' work with key aspects of both nihilism and Zen Buddhism. A basic principle of antiteleology, manifest in non-rationality, chance, specific formal techniques, and, most importantly, in the destruction of the art/life dichotomy, is the basis for my comparison of these seemingly disparate studies. I believe Zen to be much more radical and drastic than is popularly held, and, in turn, that this lineage of experimental art is more profound and spiritual than is commonly believed. Finally, I discuss in some detail the materials of each of my own compositions, as well as their philosophical ramifications, which are related to and inspired by, though by no means the same as, those discussed in the earlier part of the paper. My main artistic interest is the undermining of absolute aesthetic values, and the baffling of human conceptual and perceptual systems themselves. [Author Abstract]

52.) **Wall, J. F.**
Intermedia, hypermedia, and metamedia in Tarrare: Consumption Studies.
M.M. thesis, The University of North Carolina at Greensboro. 2013.

With my thesis, I have attempted to find a multimedia-oriented approach to musical composition that simultaneously presents a number of possible interpretations and allows for listeners to create their own. Tarrare: Consumption Studies explores a discursive space created around Tarrare, an eighteenth-century polyphagist, through instrumental music, electronic sound, spoken text, and moving image. I collaborated on many of the texts with Jensen Suther. This thesis also examines media theories that aim to address the relationships between different facets of multimedia creation and experience, particularly intermedia (a concept from Fluxus artist Dick Higgins that examines collisions between different art forms), hypermedia (a phenomenon particularly common on the Internet where different elements are explicitly linked together to form non-linear experiences), and metamedia (a process that relies on technology to take old media and rework the material into new media). I provide the text of the narration (Appendix A) and a score of the instrumental work (Appendix B). [Author Abstract]

53.) **Walley, J.**
Paracinema: Challenging medium-specificity and re-defining cinema in avant-garde film.
Ph.D. dissertation, The University of Wisconsin, Madison. 2005.

This dissertation examines paracinema, a body of artworks identified by their makers as films, and more specifically as avant-garde films, that do not employ the film medium, or reconfigure that medium so radically that the resulting works are not recognizable as films in a traditional sense. These works challenge the Modernist concept of medium-specificity, which dominates aesthetic and historical accounts of avant-garde film. These accounts hold that one of the primary aims of avant-garde filmmakers has been to explore and foreground the physical materials of the film medium. The centrality of this idea in avant-garde cinema studies has marginalized cinematic works that do not adhere to the ideals of medium-specificity, including the paracinematic works under review here. Paracinema has its basis in the longstanding tradition within the avant-garde of questioning the boundaries of art forms and the materials believed to constitute those boundaries--artistic media like painting or film. This tradition has manifested in many contexts, including certain essentialist film theories and the general tendency of expanded and inter-arts activity that can be traced from some of the original European Modernists to the post-WWII international avant-garde (e.g. happenings, Fluxus, Minimalism, Conceptual Art, and expanded cinema). After discussing several of these developments in relation to paracinema, this dissertation examines the paracinematic work of Ken Jacobs, Tony Conrad, and Anthony McCall. Each of these filmmakers, engaging the major aesthetic preoccupations of their contemporaries in film and the visual arts, were led to produce paracinema as a response to problems they imagined in the film medium and the normal modes of film exhibition and reception. The study of paracinema allows for the incorporation of previously undiscovered works by important filmmakers into the historical canon of avant-garde cinema, and demonstrates the limitations, for both artists and scholars, of a theoretical and historical account of avant-garde cinema organized around medium-specificity. This dissertation is part of an alternative account of artistic Modernism that de-emphasizes the importance of the specificity of art mediums and nuances the standard story of avant-garde film's relationship to the other arts and to Modernism in general. [Author Abstract]

54.) **Waxman, L.**
A few steps in a revolution of everyday life: Walking with the Surrealists, the Situationist International, and Fluxus.
Ph.D. dissertation, New York University. 2010.

My dissertation examines key junctures in twentieth-century artistic practice where walking has proved a central device for art making: amid the Surrealist, Situationist International, and Fluxus projects. The ambulatory tactics of these movements provide a paradigm for non-object-based art today, as exemplified by Richard Wentworth, Janet Cardiff, and Francis Al's, among others. Bipedalism has long been represented in painting, and certainly artists of past centuries have walked to scenic vistas and sketched them, but only in the twentieth century, alongside the rapprochement of art and life and the rise of performance art, has walking itself become art: witness the Surrealist itinerary, the Situationist dérive, the Fluxus walking tour. When art looks so much like life, it is critical to examine the specificity of the practice in question--walking--and how it can be used to resist dominant orders. [Author Abstract]

55.) **Weisman, S.**
The mind music of Yoko Ono: Screams and silences at the intersection of the real and the imagined.
Ph.D. dissertation, Princeton University. 2011.

John Lennon famously described Yoko Ono as "the most famous unknown artist. Everybody knows her name, but nobody knows what she does." Therefore, throughout my dissertation I use biography as a way into her music. Ono consciously uses her life as a source of inspiration in her music and her life experiences also manifest themselves in ways beyond the artist's control, so a listener who can make these connections will be able to more completely appreciate her music. By making her formative life experiences a primary focus of my dissertation, I also hope to show Ono as a modern hybrid artist. The sources of her musical philosophy, and the main influences on her work, include Japanese cultural ideas, Western avant-gardist principles, and pop (i.e., rock) sensibilities. These strands are revealed and entangled in a variety of specific works across her career. Because Ono is a controversial and polarizing figure, my first chapter presents reasons why she is worthy of a lengthy academic study. Her fame and her relationship with John Lennon have, for many, skewed her status as composer in her own right. Yet, she has been consistently pursuing music as a primary creative output since she was a child and her achievements are many. Before meeting Lennon, she already had two solo shows in the Carnegie Recital Hall, and had collaborated with eminent musicians, most notably John Cage, and later Ornette Coleman. With Lennon, she produced multiple musical projects and participated in jam sessions and concerts with some of the best-known rock stars of the era. She became the first bridge between the avant-garde and mainstream culture, which was a significant influence on many subsequent musicians. In Chapter Two, I explore Ono's status as a bridge between the East and the West, and the ways that her childhood experiences--moving between Japan and the United States and surviving the horrors of World War II--would motivate much of her art and music. For example, the title of her 1964 book, Grapefruit, a seminal work of conceptual art, is derived from her mistaken belief that the fruit was a cross between a lemon and orange, and she saw herself as a "spiritual hybrid." Her early influences would also manifest themselves in motifs that are transformed again and again throughout her career. I trace how several of these motifs--the sky, air, wind, breath, wrapping, and hiding--play out in specific works. Ono became a member of John Cage's inner circle and she has often been considered his disciple. However, this is a notion that she firmly rejects. In Chapter Three I consider Ono's relationship to the music of John Cage. While Cage's music is abstract and remotely philosophical, Ono's music became increasingly direct and emotional. This explains why she claims that expressionist twelve-tone composers, such as Arnold Schoenberg, are a more significant influence on her than Cage. In my final chapter I examine Ono's groundbreaking musical activities in the 1960s just prior to meeting Lennon. Ono helped to found and was intimately involved with Fluxus, the famed neo-Dadaist collective. Ono also organized a concert series with La Monte Young in SoHo in the 1960s, which is in now considered the beginning of downtown music, a major development in American concert music. The composition portion of my dissertation is the chamber opera Darkling for four singers and string quartet. Darkling was commissioned by American Opera Projects and premiered by them in 2006. Although Darkling is somewhat abstract, in essence, it tells the story of a newly married Jewish woman in Poland who leaves her family and sets sail for New York City before the beginning of WWII. Her life in New York is contrasted with that of family members who perished in the Holocaust. [Author Abstract]

56.) **White, A. M.**
Performed absence and a pre-formed audience: Martha Rosler's postcard novels and their implications for feminist art practice from the seventies to today.
M.A thesis, University of Southern California. 2012.

This study addresses Martha Rosler's trilogy of postcard novels and her mode of distributing them between 1974 and 1976 as a conscious decision by a woman artist to build a particular audience for her practice. The analysis centers not only on the postcards themselves, but also on the week-long gaps between them--the precise aspect of the project which cannot be reconstituted in any traditional art-viewing context. Serialization, or a play between absence and presence, ensures an engaged audience and proves to be a particularly potent strategy for women artists. To that end, this thesis involves a considered reading of the project, including the factors that led up to it: influences of performance, Fluxus, and early conceptual practices in New York in the 1960s; Martha Rosler's move to San Diego in 1968; and her resulting proximity to the West Coast women's movement. A close reading of the novels is further informed by a discussion of their primary, secondary, and tertiary modes of distribution--the mail, alternative publications, and a published book, respectively. Finally, a discussion of the critical reception and exhibition history for the novels leads to a greater understanding of their significance for Rosler's diverse oeuvre, and for the practices of artists working today. [Author Abstract]

57.)   Wolfe, H. V.
Landscapes of Dance: The 1960 Summer Workshop of Anna Halprin.
M.A. thesis, University of California, Riverside. 2012.

This thesis explores Bay Area choreographer Anna Halprin's 1960 summer workshop and affiliations with workshop participants such as Trisha Brown, Yvonne Rainer, Simone Forti, La Monte Young, and Robert Morris. I selected these particular participants because of their roles in shaping overarching fields of dance, visual arts and music. Through articulating the significance of the workshop as influential on artistic process, I frame the 1960 workshop as in concert with the larger world of the avant-garde, including Allan Kaprow's Happenings, Fluxus performances, Judson Dance Theater, Minimalist sculpture and post-war experimental music. In addition, I extend the concerns of event-based performance into the lexicon of landscape architecture by acknowledging Lawrence Halprin's role in the workshop as the architect of the deck and marital collaboration with Halprin. Eventually, he adopted scores into his architectural practice, designed scores for Halprin's dances and focused on pedestrian activities in his designs of public spaces. [Author Abstract]

58.) **Woods, N. L.**
Performing chance: Alison Knowles, Fluxus, and the enigmatic work of art.
Ph.D. dissertation, University of California, Irvine. 2010.

This dissertation turns a critical lens to the activities of the post-WWII avant-garde, with special attention paid to the international collective of visual artists, poets, musicians, and composers known as Fluxus. More specifically, I provide the first in-depth study of the aesthetic pursuits and influences of its sole founding female member, the American artist Alison Knowles, and develop a set of readings around key works created between 1962-1975. In charting Knowles's language-based notational scores and performances, objet trouvé experiments within her lived spaces, and computer-generated poems and large-scale installation projects, my approach to her practice is chronological as well as thematic. It considers important debates in the postwar era, including: the diversification of media (including the artist's body); the impact of old and new technologies (photo-documentation, film, and video); the influence of experimental music and poetry; and the emergence of performance art, feminism and liberation politics. In this way, I reconsider her production within a wider field of artistic experimentations at time when many artists were shifting toward unconventional materials and sources, and I demonstrate how Knowles's unique appropriation of chance operations and indeterminate structures engaged with publics both in and outside the rarefied space of the art world. By insisting on a participatory model of spectatorship that had the potential to change the viewing habits and relational experience enacted between artist and viewer, I argue that Knowles effectively challenged traditional notions of artistic labor and helped to redefine the field of cultural production during a time of tremendous social, political, and historical change. Ultimately, this project is a meditation on the ways in which Knowles's work, in and out of Fluxus, constitutes a provocative revaluation of twentieth-century art, one that takes the form of an exploration gender and institutions by mining the artistic possibilities of several tropes: the body, consumption, politics, and space. [Author Abstract]

59.)   **Yoshimoto, M.**
Into performance: Japanese women artists in New York, 1955--1975.
Ph.D. dissertation, Rutgers The State University of New Jersey - New Brunswick. 2002.

This dissertation considers the historical significance of five Japanese women artists--Yayoi Kusama, Yoko Ono, Takako Saito, Mieko Shiomi, and Shigeko Kubota. They were among the first Japanese women artists to leave their native country and expand their career opportunities in New York. While these artists began their careers in Japan, the conservative Japanese art world did not support women artists. By examining these five artists together for the first time, this dissertation illuminates a remarkable turning point in art history, the moment when Japanese women artists first gained recognition in the international art world. This study focuses on the years 1955-1975, the period when these five artists' paths crossed in Tokyo and New York. In both cities, these artists were active participants in avant-garde movements, thus forging a bridge between the art worlds in the East and West. With their knowledge of cutting-edge Japanese art, these artists had an impact on the early years of American performance-oriented art movements, such as Happenings and Fluxus. By discussing the role of these women artists in the development of Japanese and American art, this study revises the West-centered historical narratives of avant-garde art. While these five artists made significant contributions to the artistic exchanges between Japan and the United States, they became marginalized in histories of both countries because of their gender and ethnicity. Only recently have monographic studies appeared on Ono, Kusama, and Kubota. Saito's and Shiomi's work is absent from the art historical literature. The main goal of this study is to bring these neglected artists to light within the emerging critical context of performance art. By experimenting with a relatively new medium of performance art, these women artists rose above preconceptions about art. Through fostering interaction with spectators, they explored the expressive potential of their own bodies as a site of multiple meanings. Combining current theoretical concepts with historical documents and newly acquired artists' statements, this dissertation offers the first in-depth and interdisciplinary study of these five unique Japanese women artists. [Author Abstract]

60.) **Zimna, K.**
Play in the theory and practice of art.
Ph.D. dissertation, Loughborough University (United Kingdom). 2010.

This thesis focuses on the notion of play in the theory and practice of art in the 20th and 21st centuries. I approach play both as an `internal' element of the concept of art (following the philosophical tradition) and as the `external' model for the creative process (as applied by modern and post-modern artists). The main purpose is to produce an interpretation of play that would span various, often contradictory, features of this concept and would serve to reinterpret the notion of artistic representation, traditionally linked with the vocabulary and approaches coming from the domain of work (production, mastery, preconceived outcomes, fixity, and the nature/culture dichotomy). My thesis defends representation, however, `supplemented' with the notion of play. In my project of highlighting the role of play in the discourse of art and aesthetics, I draw on Jacques Derrida's reading of Kant and Plato. Derrida's analysis of the `logic of supplementarity' in Western thought and terms such as *parergon*, *pharmakon* and `undecidable' help me to argue that the ambivalence of play and the movement `in between' the opposites allow us to understand play as a condition of artistic representation. In terms of practice, I link the emergence of the `strategy' of play with the rhetorics of primitivism in modern avant-gardes from Dada to Fluxus. I analyse play as a tool of transgression and an `attractive supplement' of the creative process's a way to activate the public and change the traditional proper function (*ergon*) of art. I trace the assimilation of play in recent participatory (`relational dialogic') art intended to go `beyond representation' I argue that play has become a commonly used `tactic' and an undercurrent of today's artistic and social network. In the final discussion I reinterpret the notions of work (*ergon,* essence) and play (*parergon,* supplement) in the light of the 20th century artistic revolution. [Author Abstract]

Locating Dissertations and Theses

A. Purchase

Many of the dissertations and theses listed in this bibliography are available for purchase through UMI Dissertation Express:

> http://disexpress.umi.com/dxweb

By Fax:

> 800-864-0019

By Mail:

> 789 E. Eisenhower Parkway, P.O. Box 1346, Ann Arbor, Michigan 48106-1346
>
> 800-521-3042

B. Interlibrary Loan

Dissertations and theses may also be requested through Interlibrary Loan via your local public, college or university library.